DEMOCRATIC CORPORATISM
AND POLICY LINKAGES

RESEARCH SERIES/NUMBER 69

Democratic Corporatism and Policy Linkages

The Interdependence of Industrial, Labor-Market, Incomes, and Social Policies in Eight Countries

HAROLD L. WILENSKY & LOWELL TURNER

iiS

INSTITUTE
OF INTERNATIONAL
STUDIES
University of California, Berkeley

Library of Congress Cataloging-in-Publication Data

Wilensky, Harold L.
   Democratic corporatism and policy linkages.

   (Research series / Institute of International Studies,
University of Calfornia, Berkeley, ISSN 0068-6093 ;
no. 69)
   Bibliography: p.
   Includes index.
   1. Industry and state—Europe. 2. Corporate
state—Europe. 3. Europe—Politics and government—
1945- . 4. Industry and state—United States.
5. Corporate state—United States. 6. United States—
Politics and government—1945- . 7. Industry and
state—Japan. 8. Corporate state—Japan. 9. Japan—
Politics and government—1945- . I. Turner, Lowell.
II. Title. III. Series: Research series (University of
California, Berkeley. Institute of International
Studies) ; no. 69.
HD3616.E8W54 1987   338.9   87-3525
ISBN 0-87725-169-X (pbk.)

CONTENTS

Appendixes

LIST OF TABLES/CHART

ACKNOWLEDGMENTS

This monograph is a revision and expansion of a paper presented at the Thirteenth International Political Science Association World Congress, Paris, 15-20 July 1985. It is based in part on H. L. Wilensky's larger study of the political economy of taxing and spending in nineteen rich democracies. We are grateful to Thomas E. Janoski, Lloyd Ulman, and David A. Vogel for critical readings. The keen editorial eye of Bojana Ristich improved many a passage. In an early stage of the work, James M. Jasper and Susan Reed Hahn contributed helpful suggestions. Three sources of aid and comfort were indispensable: the Ford Foundation Project on Social Welfare Policy and the American Future; the Institute of International Studies (and its Director, Carl Rosberg), and the Institute of Industrial Relations (and its Director, George Strauss), University of California, Berkeley.

H. L. W.
L. T.

Berkeley, California
June 1987

INTRODUCTION

This study explores the interdependence of active labor-market, industrial, incomes, and social policies; sets them in political and economic context; and reviews literature on their implementation and effectiveness. By examining the sequence of initiation and expansion of diverse policies in each sphere, we aim to increase our understanding of their interaction and effects in eight countries chosen for contrast in the structure of their political economies: Austria, Sweden, the Netherlands, West Germany (FRG), France, Japan, the United Kingdom, and the United States.

Our central theme is that the successful implementation of policies and programs in each policy area depends upon *elite awareness* of the interdependence of public policies and *national bargaining structures* that permit top policymakers to act on this awareness. Unless elites in modern democracies grasp the interdependence of public policies and their multiple effects, they are unlikely to develop an effective policy mix to cope with the difficult constraints they have faced since the early 1970s. Even if administrative leaders and their expert advisers *are* aware of the contradictions and interacting effects of various social and economic policies, they cannot act effectively unless they are located in national bargaining structures where a wide range of issues are connected, longer-range effects are sometimes considered, and research is used for policy-planning and implementation as well as budget justification and ideological expression (Wilensky 1983). For instance, the Austrians and West Germans could not have implemented their relatively successful incomes policies unless they had in place expansive social and labor-market policies that made wage restraint tolerable to union leaders and workers. And the Japanese could not have instituted a successful industrial policy without strong structures for national collaboration among industry, commerce, and government; local collaboration

1

between management and labor, including bargaining about job security; and (as we shall see) a quite active labor-market policy—in other words, structures and policies to cushion the shocks of industrial readjustment.

Chapter 1

POLICY CLUSTERS AND THEIR DEFINITIONS

By *active labor-market policy* (ALMP) we mean direct government action to shape the *demand* for labor by maintaining or creating jobs; to increase the *supply* and *quality* of labor via training and rehabilitation; and to encourage *labor mobility* via placement, counseling, and mobility incentives. ALMP is counterposed to such passive policies as unemployment insurance and public assistance. Excluded by most students are policies that aim merely to redistribute existing work rather than increase it, such as affirmative action or coercion and bribes to eliminate older workers or immigrants from the labor market. Always excluded are measures that may affect the labor market indirectly: fiscal and monetary policy, regulation or deregulation, incomes policies, or trade and industrial policies. Programs marginal to the definition include work-sharing and regional redevelopment, which may or may not increase job or training opportunities. Of the twenty-one different programs that one can roughly fit into this definition of ALMP, sixteen comprise the core, with five others somewhat marginal (see Chart 1).

There is a wide variety of definitions in the literature on *industrial policy*; the term is often used broadly to refer to any government policies that affect industry (see Adams and Klein, eds. 1983:chs. 1 and 2 for a useful overview). We shall adopt a more restricted definition. By industrial policy we mean an organized and coherent set of policies designed to affect directly the structure of industry and thereby shape production and investment decisions. Industrial policy is concerned with adjustment, most often and increasingly to promote international competitiveness in the face of changing patterns of supply and demand.

3

Chart 1

TYPES OF PROGRAMS LABELED ACTIVE LABOR-MARKET POLICY

Government policies to create or maintain jobs (shape demand for labor)

A. Direct provision of work via

   1. sheltered workshops and other job-creation measures for handicapped workers;

   2. employment in regular public service;

   3. public works projects — e.g., building and highway construction, conservation (e.g., Civilian Conservation Corps). Proposals for National Youth Service Corps fit items 2 and 3.

B. Subsidies to private business to

   4. hire new employees;

   5. extend seasonal work year round — e.g., winter construction subsidies;

?ª 6. locate or relocate workplaces in areas of high unemployment and create new jobs (e.g., area redevelopment).

C. Laws or subsidies to maintain demand for labor via

   7. short-time work (e.g., pay workers some of the difference between part- and full-time pay to prevent layoffs);

   8. redundancy payment laws that increase the cost to employer of workforce reductions (assumes employers will be shocked into better human resource planning).

Government policies to increase the labor supply and/or improve its quality by promoting or regulating

   9. apprenticeship training;

  10. on-the-job training and retraining;

  11. work-study programs to ease transition from school to work (e.g., part-time jobs while in school so student gains orientation to work, good work habits, job experience);

12. job transition training for workers threatened with layoffs—training while still working for the same employer on the threatened job;

13. employability training—remedial programs to ijcrease basic literacy and improve work habits and attitudes.

Government policies to decrease the labor supply by

? 14. lowering the retirement age;

? 15. raising the age for compulsory schooling;

? 16. shortening the work week or reducing overtime;

? 17. reducing immigration of guest-workers or encouraging their return (through subsidies or coercion).

Government policies to encourage labor mobility via

18. placement services—labor exchanges providing job information to increase efficiency in matching job-seekers and job vacancies (can include compulsory notification of job vacancies or layoffs);

19. vocational counseling in school and during the worklife;

20. mobility allowances and relocation advice for displaced workers; "starting allowance" if search is necessary;

21. relocation assistance via housing allowances or rent supplements tied to item 20 (includes government regulation of rules for apartment waiting lists).

Sources: From Wilensky (1985:2). Based on Janoski (1986), Reubens (1970), and Lester (1966).

[a]Question mark indicates a program marginal to the definition of ALMP but included by some students.

Included in this definition are sectoral policies to promote growth industries, manage declining industries, encourage research and development and the spread of advanced technology in industry, and promote competitiveness by encouraging mergers and/or domestic competition. Excluded are broad fiscal and monetary policies; labor-market and wage policies; health, safety, and environmental policies; and other policies which affect industry in a non-selective way (such as general tax breaks and investment incentives—sometimes called "horizontal industrial policies"). In the gray area are regional development policies that restructure industry geographically but do not necessarily change the sectoral composition of a nation's industry or affect its competitive adjustment (e.g., the separate and competing subsidies for industrial relocation adopted by some states of the United States).

Common policy instruments can be indicative (national plans or voluntary agreements between authorities and private firms) or coercive and "coercive-persuasive" (price controls, technical standards, tariffs, quotas, export financing, subsidies to research and development, selective tax credits, preferential credits, guaranteed loans, public purchases, service facilities).

By *incomes policies* we mean government policies to hold down general wage levels by affecting directly the process by which wage levels are set. The purpose may vary: for example, to reduce the rate of inflation (when the labor market is tight), decrease unemployment (when the labor market is loose), or promote growth without increasing inflation or unemployment. The most common short-term goal is to reduce the rate of change of nominal wages.

Included are government wage guidelines (whether legally enforceable or not), "jawboning," mandatory wage freezes and controls, and government involvement (either openly or behind the scenes) in bipartite or tripartite wage bargaining. Excluded are policies designed to raise wages or to set minimum wage levels. Also excluded are policies which may indirectly affect wage levels, such as fiscal and monetary policies or legislation that weakens the power of labor unions.

Incomes policies are often counterposed to deflationary policies as an alternative method of achieving wage restraint. The former (it is claimed) can hold down inflation without increasing unemployment and reducing output; deflationary policies hold down inflation at the cost of unemployment and low growth.

Closely associated with incomes policies are the tradeoffs labor gets in return for lower wage increases. These include social transfers, tax changes, ALMP, employment security, institutional security for unions, and—most commonly—accompanying price controls or the promise of price restraint.

Incomes policies did not emerge as a major instrument of macroeconomic policy until the 1960s.

Social policy is a diffuse, residual category, sometimes as broad as three quarters of what governments do, sometimes as narrow as income maintenance for the poor. For our purposes, we will consider it as roughly equivalent to the "welfare state" (Wilensky 1975). Because the core programs of the welfare state— pensions and disability insurance, health insurance, family allowances, job injury insurance, unemployment insurance, miscellaneous aid to the poor and handicapped—generally preceded the three policy clusters we have discussed (in Europe, for instance, almost all of them were in place by World War I)—we will not try to sort out the sequence of initiation and change (for that see Flora and Heidenheimer, eds. 1981 and Wilensky et al. 1985). Instead we will use contrasts in and expansion of aggregate social-security spending as a proxy for social-policy development in these eight countries. Despite obvious national differences in program emphasis and sector spending (Wilensky 1975:105-7) and differences in ideological justification, the effort a country makes to deal with the problems of the aged via public pensions and related programs is tightly and increasingly related to its effort in family allowances and related family policies, as well as work-injury insurance and related efforts in occupational safety and health. For various reasons, health-insurance spending is less closely related to the rest of this package, means-tested public assistance is unrelated, and higher education spending is inversely related to the rest (based on a nineteen-country analysis of the mid-1960s and 1970s by Wilensky, unpublished data). Since World War II and at the extremes represented by these eight countries, the welfare-state leaders (measured by social-security spending/GNP) tend to adopt and expand a great range of social policies that increase the security of their people and thereby make industrial and incomes policies less threatening, while the welfare-state laggards, providing less of a "social wage," expose their populations to greater risks. Why Japan is only a partial exception will be discussed below.

Chapter 2

THE POLICY CONTEXT:
THREE BROAD TYPES OF POLITICAL ECONOMY

As we try to sort out national differences in labor-market, industrial, incomes, and social policies and assess their interaction, implementation, and effects, we must first place these policies firmly in political and economic context. Unless we specify variations in the structure of modern political economies, we cannot assess the validity of general assertions about the fiscal crisis of "the" welfare state, the prospects of economic ruin, the collapse of consensus (Janowitz 1976), the decline of the capacity to govern (King 1975; Rose and Peters 1978), or the various scenarios and tradeoffs suggested in the literature on social and industrial policy. The very definition of economic and political constraints on public policy depends on which of three types of market-oriented democracies we are talking about. We shall label them democratic corporatist, corporatist without labor, and least corporatist.*

*Wilensky's version of neo-corporatism (1976 and 1983) draws on work by Schmitter (1974) and related themes from discussions of "consociational democracy" (Lijphart 1968; Daalder 1974). In such collections of essays on corporatism as Schmitter and Lehmbruch, eds. (1979), Lehmbruch and Schmitter, eds. (1982), and Berger, ed. (1981), there is much conceptual muddiness and with rare exceptions (e.g., Schmidt 1982; Schmitter 1981; Kriesi 1982), little effort to frame propositions for systematic tests. For instance, there is a strong tendency to mix up attributes of structures (e.g., degrees of centralization or bureaucratization or oligarchy), processes of policymaking (e.g., stages of decisionmaking); the content of particular policies and programs (e.g., incomes policy), policy implementation (effective or ineffective), or effects (good or poor economic performance, more or less equality). As a result, it is impossible to relate corporatism as structural attributes of political economy to policy processes, content, implementation, and impact. This conceptual confusion intensifies the already severe difficulties of data collection and cross-national comparability familiar to everyone. It accounts for the lack of agreement about which countries qualify as "corporatist."

9

The first type, consisting of such countries as Austria, Sweden, Norway, Finland, Belgium, the Netherlands, and perhaps West Germany, has four interrelated characteristics: (1) a bargaining structure for arriving at consensus leading to (2) a blurring of public and private spheres which fosters (3) a wide scope of national bargaining (increasing the possibility of a more-or-less effective social contract) in which (4) social policy is absorbed into general economic policy, thereby strengthening chances for consensus, and so on. A word about each:

1. The structure for consensual bargaining provides for the interplay of strongly organized, usually centralized interest groups, especially labor, employer, and professional associations, with a centralized or moderately centralized government obliged by law or informal agreement to consider their advice.

2. The peak bargains struck by such federations reflect and further a blurring of old distinctions between the public and the private. Private bargaining and collective government decisions in corporatist democracies such as Sweden, Austria, Norway, and the Netherlands are difficult to separate. For instance, the Dutch Foundation of Labor, a nonprofit institution for central deliberations of employer and labor federations, runs parallel to the powerful Social and Economic Council, a tripartite institution for collegial accommodations seldom ignored by the government. Norway's "voluntary" organizations on a national level have official status to negotiate with government or opposing interest groups; they receive subsidies for their activities as a political right. Sometimes these agreements are bilateral (e.g., the Ministry of Education negotiates with the authors' association about government grants and living stipends); sometimes they are trilateral (e.g., in industrial relations centralized, compulsory arbitration is the rule).

3. The scope of bargaining is wide; the tradeoffs among bargaining parties encompass a wide range of national issues. These quasi-public associations therefore have a chance to produce what eluded Prime Minister Harold Wilson, what Prime Minister James Callaghan officially pronounced dead, and what is alien to Prime Minister Margaret Thatcher: an effective social

contract. Their struggle for consensus is not narrowly focused on the labor market—wages, hours, working conditions—as it has been in the United Kingdom, Canada, the United States, or even Denmark. The consensus may or may not involve a formal plan (as in French or Norwegian "indicative planning"). It may or may not involve high rates of membership in unions (the percentage is medium in the Netherlands, low in France). It certainly does not require or result in "the detailed administrative running of the economy" (G.K. Wilson 1982:232). *What counts are channels for influence for top leaders of economic interest groups meeting in the broadest national context.*

4. Social policy is in some measure absorbed into general economic policy. One reason for the relative effectiveness of this type of consensus is that the big issues are economic growth, prices, wages, taxes, unemployment, trade, and the balance of payments; welfare, housing, health care, and social security are absorbed into these broad discussions. Such an integration of economic and social policy tends toward an important result: at a time of slow growth and rising aspirations, labor, interested in wages and social security, is forced to take account of inflation, productivity, and the need for investment; employers, interested in profit, productivity, and investment, are forced to take account of social policy; both labor and management are forced to take account of government concern with economic performance, tax revenues, and the balance of payments.

To illustrate the nature of tradeoffs facilitated by such consensus-making machines, consider two cases (based on interviews with a few of the main actors). The first is an example of typical tradeoffs comprising an economic package. In Norway in the late 1970s labor, management, and government reached an agreement in which labor got a 3 percent increase in real wages (involving a realistic constraint on nominal wages), including government subsidies to fishermen and farmers, in return for a cut in profits taxes on industry. The second case suggests that corporatist bargaining arrangements do not depend on the continuity of Left party power. In Sweden from the early

1950s to the mid-1960s the top leaders of the Social Democrats, the labor federations, and the Federation of Swedish Industry met privately at the summer home of the prime minister to work out national economic and social policy. As the system became institutionalized and media coverage became more prominent, the informal private meetings continued, but agreements were ritually affirmed at a country estate called Harpsund, donated to the state by a private industrialist. By the 1970s these bargaining customs became known as "Harpsund democracy." When the "bourgeois bloc" took over in 1976, the system continued; only the faces changed—and some observers tagged it "Haga democracy" after the royal palace preferred as a meeting place by the new Fälldin government. A 1978 Swedish bargain included a government-desired increase in the value-added tax designed to dampen inflation and debt by cutting consumption. Labor viewed it as regressive but accepted it in return for an increase in family allowances to offset the tax burden for large, relatively poor families. The defeat of the Social Democrats did not change the essential machinery.

In short, democratic corporatism as a structure for bargaining does not predetermine either the issues to be joined or the content of agreements. Nothing in logic or practice blocks *any* issue from discussion and resolution.

For a classification of nineteen rich democracies by their fit to this model of corporatism and measures of corporatism, see Wilensky (1976 and 1981:367). These scores cannot capture ambiguities in two or three cases, especially West Germany. Most important for our discussion here, they do not capture the second type of corporatism that we find useful for our analysis of the interplay of structure and policy as well as the degree of policy integration—i.e., *corporatism without full-scale participation by labor* (see Pempel and Tsunekawa 1979).

Japan, France, and perhaps Switzerland in varying ways have developed quasi-public bargaining structures for the interplay of industry, commerce, agriculture, professional groups, and government. These structures permit some coordination and planning of social and economic policies, but they have so far kept labor federations at a distance. In all three countries, despite obvious differences in the strength of the state bureaucracy, the business community enjoys a privileged position in the definition and implementation of public policy. These countries are thus in a position to achieve good economic performance without adopting many public policies explicitly designed to increase economic and social equality. In view of the urgency of mass demands and the severity of economic constraints, however, these three countries may one day be forced to move toward the full incorporation of labor into their bargaining arrangements, eventually joining the first group. The election of François Mitterrand in France might have signaled a move in this direction, but the ideological and structural splits between Communist and non-Communist unions immensely complicated the process, and it never got off the ground. Indeed with fewer local notables and businessmen in parliament; with the breakup of the coalition of farmers (FNSEA), business (CNPF), and the bureaucratic-political elite; and with the replacement of over half of the directors in the ministries, France may have experienced more erosion of corporatism-without-labor under Mitterrand than integration of labor into the system. The conservative victory of 1986 has further diminished the prospect of labor inclusion. If these countries do not move toward inclusion of labor, they may swing toward authoritarianism—the increasing use of coercion to control a rising level of organized discontent focused on equality and security.

The strains within government-industry style corporatism are evident in variations in the effectiveness of conflict resolution by policy areas in Japan. It is apparent that the machinery for consensus in economic and industrial policy (Johnson 1982) works far more effectively than it does for social and environmental policies, which are further from the central concerns of the bargaining parties. For instance, the marks of Japanese corporatism so prominent in the interaction of the Ministry of Trade and Industry (MITI), the Finance Ministry, the ruling Liberal Democratic Party, and industry and trade associations in shaping economic policy—decisions by consensus, bureaucratic dominance, long- or at least medium-range plans, assertion of national interests—are almost wholly absent in the history of pension development, especially from the 1959 National Pension System to today's pension crisis. Japan's pension system was conceived in acrimonious controversy that continues to this day, with labor unions, farmers, employers, the insurance industry, the finance ministry, the ministry of welfare, and political parties fighting it out, their positions very similar to those of their counterparts in the United States (Wilensky 1984).

Similarly, Japanese corporatism was extraordinarily unresponsive to mounting environmental pollution and the mass protests that accompanied it. During the 1950s and early 1960s the government ignored noxious air pollution over industrial cities as well as localized outbreaks of horrifying diseases rooted in pollution. For instance, in the celebrated case of deaths and disability from mercury poisoning in the fish eaten by residents of Minamata, the home of the Japan Chisso (nitrogen) Company, it took fifteen years before the victims or their families received compensation. Intense public pressure, including a growing environmental movement, media coverage, law suits, and American-style mass protests and demonstrations, culminated in the 1970 "Pollution Diet," which passed more than a dozen laws. In 1971 the government set up an environmental agency. Between 1971 and 1973 four major court decisions imposed stiff fines and standards of negligence on industrial polluters (McKean 1980; Enloe 1975). It was only then that the usual machinery—the powerful ministries (MITI, the Ministry of Finance, the Ministry of Construction, and the Ministry of Transportation), the top leaders of the ruling party, with industry as a reluctant partner—swung into action. The government offered big depreciation allowances; government banks provided low-interest loans for pollution control; MITI helped finance research and development in pollution-control technology; standards were high, penalties severe. In general, the action was quick and effective; the air in Tokyo, once the filthiest in the world, is today quite clean; given the depth of risk (a highly dense industrial population), other environmental hazards have been impressively reduced. The lesson: countries in this second category are slow to respond to mass pressures (from labor, environmental, and similar groups), but once they decide to respond, they can easily and swiftly implement the new policies. (Compare Love Canal in the United States: much agitation and saturation media coverage, resulting in quick state action to move residents out and quick compensation of victims, with no sustained national followthrough.)

The third category includes countries that are least corporatist in their bargaining structures—the fragmented and decentralized political economies of the United States, the United Kingdom, Canada, and Australia, none of which are advanced welfare states. In these countries, the interest groups that elsewhere are constrained by the necessity of national bargaining and tradeoffs are in a position to act out their most parochial strivings, reinforcing an already advanced state of paralysis.

As this account suggests, nothing is static; many observers claim that the Netherlands, once a model of democratic corporatism, is losing its capacity to forge consensus, and recent literature is full of assertions that the structures for centralized bargaining in Sweden are breaking up. Whatever the variations and ambiguities over space and time, we would argue that without structures for bargaining approximating the model of corporatism we have specified, the minimum consensus essential for effective coordination of contradictory social, industrial, labor, and economic policies is unlikely for any rich democracy in the years ahead. In an increasingly unfavorable economic environment, the corporatist democracies listed above have a chance to arrive at such consensus because they already have in place channels for bargaining and influence for top leaders of economic interest groups meeting in the broadest national context.

Now let us apply this scheme to four policy clusters in the eight countries noted in the introduction. The countries are chosen for their fit to the model and for availability of data after World War II in all policy areas. Three are clearly corporatist—Austria, Sweden, the Netherlands; one is marginal—West Germany.* Two are corpora-

---

*Measures of the centralization of labor federations and government do not capture some tendencies in the West German political economy. Structurally, while the central labor federation, the Deutschergewerkschaftsbund (DGB), is relatively weak and there are important elements of decentralization in government, it can be argued that functional equivalents of corporatism would justify a higher score (Wilensky 1976:51): industry-wide bargaining by moderately centralized unions informally coordinating their strategy, the growing professionalization of union staffs, the wage leadership of the metal workers, the presence of a big employer association, much centralized bargaining in the health industry, etc. During the decade of the "Konzierte Aktion" especially, German unions traded off wage restraint for other nonwage gains (e.g., the growth of works councils) (compare Lehmbruch 1979 and Streeck 1978, 1983). Although West Germany is an ambiguous case of corporatism, it is included in our analysis because it is active in all four policy areas.

tist without labor—Japan and France. The United States and the United Kingdom are least corporatist.

Chapter 3

THE INTERDEPENDENCE OF POLICIES

In Appendix A we have summarized the major policy developments since World War II in each of three areas. From this chronology and the literature on which it is based, we infer the degree of elite commitment to the policy area and policy persistence or continuity, and arrive at what we consider informed speculation about the degree of policy success. (As we suggested above, we report only broad spending patterns as a clue to social policy development although we have examined specific social policies as well.)

By examining the sequence of initiation and expansion of diverse policies in each policy domain, we aim to test two general propositions:

1. The adoption and expansion of industrial and incomes policies as well as their successful implementation depend on the simultaneous or prior development of active labor-market and/or social policies. The latter permit the sharing of burdens and benefits of industrial and incomes policies in ways most voters and/or organized labor see as fair or at least tolerable.

2. In both elite perceptions and action, public-policy linkages are strongest where the structure of the political economy is corporatist. Specifically,

   a. Corporatist democracies that fully include labor in their policymaking and implementation are most likely to evidence the interdependence of the four clusters of policies.

   b. Corporatist democracies that keep labor at a distance from major policy decisions are most likely to adopt industrial and/or incomes policies before they expand ALMP and social policies, but if industrial and incomes policies are to be

17

sustained and effective, they will sooner or later be accompanied by policy payoffs in these other areas.

c. Least-corporatist political economies are not likely to develop policy linkages that permit the mobilization of mass support through necessary tradeoffs, nor will they develop the continuity of policy through different regimes that enhances program effectiveness. Fragmented and decentralized structures for bargaining among major economic power blocs produce extreme policy segmentation in which both policy deliberation and policy research are confined to separate compartments, a zero-sum mentality among competing interest groups is prominent, and continuity of policy is minimized.

Our reading of the record generally affirms these hypotheses and pinpoints partial exceptions. Table 1 provides a summary overview.

Regarding the relation of corporatism to public-policy linkages (leaving aside the question of sequence), three of the four corporatist democracies—Austria, Sweden, and the FRG—show very strong interdependence of all four policy domains. The Netherlands appears to be a partial exception. It evidenced a tight integration of all areas beginning in the reconstruction period in 1945, with continuing linkage within a tripartite framework through the 1950s. After 1950 industrial policy receded, while incomes and labor-market policies continued. There was a turning point around 1962, when social policy showed a sharp expansion (e.g., social security spending/GNP up from 12.8 percent in 1962 to 18.3 percent in 1966) while incomes policy weakened greatly, collapsing by the early 1970s, when unions and employers could no longer agree on a wide range of issues. Social policy, however, had a life of its own and continued its sharp expansion. As structures for big-bloc bargaining weakened, policy linkages weakened. In short, tight policy integration in the first half of the postwar period gave way to some policy segmentation in the last half. The rank for the whole period, medium, makes the Netherlands the exception that proves the rule.

The two cases of corporatism without labor fit the notion that such systems do not need as much policy linkage of deep interest to labor, especially dependence on social policy (Japan rates low;

Table I

CORPORATISM, POLICY INTERDEPENDENCE, SOCIAL SPENDING (SS), QUALITATIVE RANKS OF
SUCCESS, AND ECONOMIC PERFORMANCE INDICATORS IN EIGHT COUNTRIES, 1950-74, 1975-79, AND 1980-84

Type of Political Economy and Country	Rank for Interdependence (All 4 Policy Areas)	SS/GNP, 1950-74 (Percent & Rank)	SS/GNP, 1977-79 (Percent & Rank)	Qualitative Rank of Effort and Success				Economic Performance Indicators											
				ALMP	Industrial Policy	Incomes Policy	Composite Rank, 3 Areas	1950-74				1975-79				1980-84			
								Unemployment	Growth	Inflation	Sum. Econ. Performance	Unemployment	Growth	Inflation	Sum. Econ. Performance	Unemployment	Growth	Inflation	Sum. Econ. Performance
Corporatist																			
Austria	H[a]	19.3(H)	24.5(H)	4	4	1	3.5	2.2(M)	4.6(H)	5.3(M)	G[b]	1.8(L)	2.4(H)	5.7(L)	E	3.2(L)	1.6(M)	5.3(L)	E
Sweden	H	15.5(H-M)	30.6(H)	1	5	3	3.5	1.7(L)	3.2(M)	5.1(M)	G	1.9(L)	0.2(L)	13.3(M+)	F	2.8(L)	1.4(M)	9.5(M)	G
Netherlands	M+	15.5(H-M)	30.1(H)	5	6	5	6	1.8(L)	3.8(M)	5.0(M)	G	4.0(M)	1.6(L)	7.9(L)	F	10.7(H)	-0.3(L)	4.3(L)	FP
Germany West	H	18.9(H)	26.2(H)	2	3	2	1	2.6(M)	4.7(H)	3.8(L)	E	3.6(M)	2.6(H)	4.4(L)	E	6.3(M)	1.0(M)	3.7(L)	G
Corporatist without labor																			
Japan	M	5.1(L)	8.6(L)	3	1	4	2	1.7(L)	8.0(H)	5.7(H)	G	1.9(L)	3.8(H)	5.9(L)	E	2.4(L)	3.3(H)	2.0(L)	E
France	M-	17.4(H)	28.0(H)	6	2	6	5	2.4(M)	4.2(H)	5.8(H)	F	4.6(M)	2.6(H)	10.4(M)	G	7.9(M)	0.6(L)	10.7(H)	P
Least corporatist																			
United Kingdom	M-	12.7(M)	15.8(L)	8	7	7	7	2.7(M)	2.3(L)	5.0(M)	FP	4.5(M)	1.9(ML)	16.4(H)	FP	9.5(H)	0.5(L)	9.6(M)	P
United States	L	7.9(L)	14.8(L)	7	8	8	8	5.2(H)	2.4(L)	3.2(L)	G	6.8(H)	2.8(H)	6.9(L)	G	8.2(M+)	0.9(M)	6.7(L)	G

Sources: See Appendix B for measures of economic performance and social spending.

[a] The ranks are as follows: H=high; M=medium; L=low.

[b] The composite index of economic performance (see Appendix B) weighs each of three measures equally for a composite rank of E=excellent (low unemployment, high growth, low inflation); G=good; F=fair; P=poor.

France, high). The least-corporatist countries, the United Kingdom and United States (discussed below) fit the expected pattern; policy linkages, while apparent in some years of UK history, tend to be weak in both countries and policy continuity, limited.

Regarding hypothesis 1, about sequences of initiation and expansion, the record yields strong support. None of the eight countries either initiates or expands and sustains an *industrial policy* without (a) preceding or simultaneous initiation and expansion of *ALMP* (Japan, the Netherlands, Sweden, West Germany), and/or (b) preceding or simultaneous initiation and expansion of *social policy* (Austria, France, the Netherlands, Sweden, West Germany). The emphasis varies from country to country. In Japan, for example, industrial policy gets more weight than ALMP, while in Sweden the reverse is true. Nonetheless, the pattern of interdependence and sequence is clear. Countries unable (United Kingdom) or unwilling (United States) to sustain an organized and coherent industrial policy are not, of course, part of the pattern. If nothing is done, or something is tried and quickly abandoned, sequence is not relevant. It can be argued, however, that the United Kingdom has a bit more linkage than the United States because its industrial policy and ALMP efforts generally rise and fall together in a stop-and-go pattern.

France, which made little use of ALMP while developing a major industrial policy in the immediate postwar period, did, however, expand social policies. Beginning with an edict issued 4 October 1945, it revamped its entire social-security system at a critical juncture in the early development of industrial policy. An unusual coalition of the Mouvement Républicain Populaire (Catholic in ideology) and the Communist and Socialist parties by April 1946 had replaced a rather patchy system of private and cooperative schemes with wide public coverage against sickness, accidents, and old age, reinforced by a generous system of family allowances (Hanley, Kerr, and Waites 1979:2; Laroque, ed. 1983). The subsequent and parallel expansion of both social and industrial policies fits our hypothesis. Successful industrial readjustment appears to require the flexibility and cushioning of either ALMP, social policies, or both.

In a similar fashion, none of the eight countries either initiates or expands and sustains an *incomes policy* without (a) preceding or simultaneous initiation and expansion of *ALMP* (Japan, the

Netherlands, Sweden, West Germany, United Kingdom), and/or (b) preceding or simultaneous expansion of *social policy* (Austria, the Netherlands, Sweden, West Germany). Again, the shape and weight of the policies vary. In Japan de facto incomes policy is linked informally with other policies, while in Austria a formal incomes policy is a central component of government economic policy. Countries that do not fit the pattern—the United States and France—have had only limited and short-term success in the implementation of incomes policies. In the United Kingdom major incomes policy efforts (with only short-term success) have risen and fallen with ALMP and industrial policy, as British governments alternate. Successful, sustained incomes policy, whether de facto or explicit, appears to require the tradeoff and cushioning effect of either ALMP, social policy, or both.

In the two corporatist political economies with little integration of labor into policymaking and implementation—France and Japan—industrial policy dominates the other three policy areas. Nonetheless, Japan made use of limited ALMP (with an active placement service) during its industrial policy expansion in the 1950s and increased its use of ALMP during the shift to readjustment in the 1970s. France expanded social policies after the war as indicative planning became a dominant strategy, and it later adopted ALMP as industrial planners encountered the need for readjustment in the 1970s. Although tradeoffs between social and labor policies, on the one hand, and industrial and incomes policies, on the other hand, appear less necessary in these countries, the pattern remains.

The two least-corporatist countries show the most policy fragmentation and discontinuity. There is, as noted, a consistency of failed interdependence in the United Kingdom's stop-and-go pattern. In 1948-50 a short-lived incomes policy was linked to the expansion of the welfare state; in 1961 short-lived attempts at incomes and industrial policies were linked; subsequent expansion and contraction in ALMP, incomes, and industrial policies were accompanied by a modest expansion in social policy. Although all four areas were cut back together in 1979-80, ALMP was again expanded after 1980 as the Thatcher government continued to cut education budgets but rediscovered vocational training (see McArthur and McGregor 1986).

With its dominant free-market ideology and decentralized

structure, the United States has made sustained use of neither industrial nor incomes policy. It is an extreme case which confirms our assumption that even where leaders are aware of the imperatives of policy linkages and try to act, implementation is unlikely without appropriate structures for bargaining and implementation. Consider a quarter-century effort to engineer the obvious tradeoffs that would reduce dependence on tariffs as a means to resist import injury. In 1962 President John F. Kennedy proposed a program called Trade Adjustment Assistance (TAA), designed to give workers a way out of import-sensitive industries and reduce political opposition to free trade. As passed by Congress, TAA combined training to upgrade skills of workers threatened by foreign competition, relocation benefits, and income maintenance with a uniform national standard. President George Meany of the ALF-CIO, departing from the frequent protectionism of American labor, strongly supported the program.

The story of implementation is one of dashed hopes. For seven years not a single TAA petition was approved by the Tariff Commission. When during the next several years eligibility rules were relaxed, only about 35,000 workers received assistance, very few of whom received training. By 1973 the AFL-CIO complained of broken promises, and protectionism was on the rise again. Congress, against the wishes of the Nixon administration, improved the authorizing legislation. It set up a new trust fund which used tariff revenue to pay for the costs of worker adjustment, instituted a job-search benefit, increased adjustment assistance, and moved the certification process to a presumably more labor-oriented agency, the Department of Labor (DOL).

Again, implementation was slow and violations of rules on timing and support were common. This time state employment agencies, responsible for outreach and delivery of benefits, failed to follow through. Both the DOL and the states lacked the funds, the data base, and the competence necessary for implementation of the training, counseling, and relocation provisions. Further, while there may be a national interest in relocating workers, states charged with service delivery may doubt that depopulation is in their interest. At no point in this long history was there an effort to mobilize natural constituencies among unions, industries, and communities to make the program work. By 1976, when President Gerald Ford reduced tariffs in four "import-injured" industries and announced that he would expedite TAA petitions, both labor and industry had soured on the program and were looking out after their own protection, screaming for more trade barriers. The program had become a purely income-maintenance effort. Under President Jimmy Carter such income-assistance costs climbed sharply because of layoffs in the automobile industry; training continued to decline.

The inevitable cost-benefit analysts now closed in. In 1979 and 1980 evaluation researchers pronounced the TAA program ineffective: income maintenance was a disincentive to job search, recipients did not improve their labor-market position relative to the recipients of unemployment compensation, etc. What the researchers ignored were the original purposes of TAA—to link training and mobility assistance to trade policy and thereby reduce political opposition to freer trade. They also ignored structural and budgetary barriers to implementation.

Under President Ronald Reagan, the TAA program was redesigned to cut costs; the legislative history of 1981 suggests that Congress was even unaware of the dormant training requirement in the 1962 law. By 1983 the administration was proposing to abolish the program. (For a detailed account, see Charnovitz 1986.) In 1987, after six years of mounting protectionist sentiment and action, the Reagan administration finally endorsed an expanded but still modest worker assistance and training program; it proposed to abolish the TAA as a quid pro quo.

The structural barriers to effective policy linkage and implementation are plain: the division of powers between the executive branch and Congress; the incapacity of administrative agencies to link trade policy and ALMP; the complexities of federal-state relations; the lack of institutionalized channels through which the main actors can resolve conflict, feed back intelligence, and participate in policy, implementation, and outreach. In short, even where the federal government has the awareness and the will, in the absence of appropriate bargaining structures, policy fails.

Chapter 4

ESTIMATES OF SUCCESS,
QUALITATIVE AND QUANTITATIVE

There is much talk about the success or failure of each cluster of policies we have considered. In the literature cited there are occasionally systematic efforts to estimate the economic impact of industrial policies in two or more countries (Magaziner and Reich 1982; Zysman and Tyson 1984; Adams and Klein, eds. 1983), incomes policies (Flanagan, Soskice, and Ulman 1983; Fallick and Elliot, eds. 1981; and Katzenstein 1985), and ALMP (Scharpf 1981, 1983; Johanneson and Schmid 1980; Haveman 1982; Haveman and Saks 1985; Casey and Bruche 1985). For three obvious reasons it is difficult to assess the success or failure of these policies with any precision. First, both scholars and practitioners articulate diverse and sometimes conflicting goals for each type of policy. Second, methods of policy evaluation differ—from narrow econometric studies of easily quantified outcomes (such as inflation effects) to qualitative historical accounts of the effects of various policy mixes on social consensus or political legitimacy. Finally—and this is the central theme of this monograph—particular policies or even clusters of policies will have one effect when considered alone, another when considered in relation to all relevant policies. For instance, none of these policies—labor-market, industrial, or incomes—can be viewed as substitutes for fiscal and monetary policies, and the net effect of any one of them depends on its interaction with the rest. In the case of the United States no national industrial policy, no incomes policy, no package of social and labor-market policies can overcome the handicaps of an overvalued dollar (from mid-1980 until February 1985), huge trade deficits, and a domestic economy disrupted by credit crunches and recessions every three or four years. Similarly, the recent decline in the value of the dollar (since February 1985) will not by itself solve persistent national problems of industrial readjustment and competitiveness in the absence of effectively linked policy clusters.

Nevertheless, our reading of the literature suggests a few recurrent themes that justify an impressionistic rank-order of the degree of success in implementation—inferences for each country regarding the political and administrative resources it devotes to each policy area, persistence of elite commitment, and achievement of at least the main goals all the countries appear to share. We generated a qualitative judgment first and then compared relevant quantitative data on inflation, unemployment, and real growth in GDP per capita, averaging annual rates for three periods: from 1950 to 1974, after the first oil shock from 1975 to 1979, and after the second oil shock from 1980 to 1984. Where authors disagreed about success, we made judgments of the relative merits of data and arguments. To validate the qualitative rankings we compared them with the average economic performance of each country for long periods to smooth out short-term fluctuations and to capture cumulative effects; most of these policies are designed to deal with long-run problems of adjustment anyway. The post-1974 period is divided to capture adaptation to massive external shocks. Performance during 1975-79 should capture the speed and strength of readjustment after the Arab oil embargo of December 1973; performance during 1980-84 should capture adjustment to the oil shock of 1979 and the concurrent interest-rate shock—generated by Paul Volcker of the U.S. Federal Reserve—which was self-administered for the United States but external for other countries.

SUMMARY RANKS AND ECONOMIC PERFORMANCE

ACTIVE LABOR-MARKET POLICY

Although the goals of ALMP include equality (improving the situation of the most disadvantaged), the reduction of skill shortages and production bottlenecks, the improvement of worklife productivity, and even the control of inflation (Rehn 1985; Wilensky 1985), the dominant goal, with strongest mass support, is to reduce unemployment. Table 2 therefore aligns average unemployment rates next to our qualitative ranks. For details see Appendix A; a few summary comments will suffice here.

Table 2

ACTIVE LABOR-MARKET POLICY (ALMP):
QUALITATIVE RANK AND UNEMPLOYMENT RATES

Summary Ranking of Successful Implementation of ALMP Inferred from Literature	Average Annual Unemployment Rates[a] *(Percent and Rank)*		
	1950-74	1975-79	1980-84
1. Sweden	1.7% (L)	1.9% (L)	2.8% (L)
2. West Germany	2.6 (M)	3.6 (M)	6.3 (M)
3. Japan	1.7 (L)	1.9 (L)	2.4 (L)
4. Austria	2.2 (L)	1.8 (L)	3.2 (L)
5. Netherlands	1.8 (L)	4.0 (M)	10.7 (H)
6. France	2.4 (ML)	4.6 (MH)	7.9 (MH)
7. United States	5.2 (H)	6.8 (H)	8.2 (MH)
8. United Kingdom	2.7 (M)	4.5 (MH)	9.5 (H)
Average for nineteen rich democracies	2.9	3.9	6.8

[a]For sources, see Appendix B.

Except for West Germany in all periods and the United Kingdom in the first period, the qualitative rankings of success essentially match the unemployment rates; countries highest in resource commitment and most successful in implementation show the lowest long-term unemployment rates and vice versa. In sophistication, resource commitment, and policy continuity, as well as success in reducing unemployment, *Sweden* is unrivaled. Its combination of job training, job creation, placement services, and mobility incentives has clearly helped keep unemployment low even as industry adjusts and even when economic growth has been slow and inflation high (as in the 1970s). During the second half of the 1970s the estimated net effect on unemployment (i.e., point reduction of potential unemployment) averaged 3.2 percent in Sweden compared to 1.3 percent in West Germany (Scharpf 1981: 29; Haveman 1982; Rehn 1985; Johanneson and Schmid 1980; Schmidt 1982). The difference parallels the expenditures in the two countries for ALMP in 1978, a year of West German cutbacks: 2.4 percent of GNP for Sweden, .50 percent for West Germany (Wilensky 1985:6). That *West Germany* has a somewhat higher unemployment rate for all three periods than its summary rank warrants may be partly explained by fluctuation in resource commitment and partly by its policy mix: it relies more on wage subsidies to keep or hire redundant workers and less on training and job creation (Johanneson and Schmid 1980:400-401); arguably the former are less effective in the long run. Still, West Germany ranks high because of its consistently successful placement service, extensive apprenticeship programs, and (until recently) training programs, as well as its successful job-creation effort in the 1970s. However, ALMP was further cut back in the 1980s, at a time of greatest need, and the government has failed to combine ALMP with other policies to prevent high and persistent unemployment.

Like Sweden and West Germany, third-ranked *Japan* has a strong labor-market board. By the early 1960s Japan had reached its goal of full employment. By 1965 the Public Employment Security Offices, with an extensive network of offices throughout the country, accounted for 70 percent of all placements. By 1970 Japan was spending .4 percent of GNP on ALMP—less effort than Sweden, the United Kingdom, and West Germany, but more than the United States (OECD 1974:53). The accent was on training, retraining, and mobility incentives. In the mid-1970s a major expansion began, embracing subsidies for employment adjustment for industrial restructuring, vocational training (including training allowances, job search and moving expenses, and targeted subsidies for employers who hire and/or train hard-to-employ groups and workers displaced by industrial restructuring), and an employment stabilization fund—countercyclical subsidies to deal with temporary layoffs and training—as well as public works. Government policies serve as backup for continual enterprise training.

After the 1973-74 oil shock Japan made a remarkably quick employment adjustment; full employment with low inflation was maintained through the 1970s. Although job training is mainly internal to the large firms, ALMP supplements the enterprise-based employment system (Shimada 1980:21), and there is good coordination among employers, unions, workers, and the government bureaucracy (Shimada 1980:27; Levine 1983:43). Among other sources of success were the following: employers' willingness to invest in human resources in the one fourth to one third of the economy dominated by large and growing firms with low interfirm mobility; a strong basic education system on which job training can build; extreme labor-market segmentation; and pressure on women and older workers to leave jobs in hard times (Cole 1979; Rohlen 1979; Shimada 1977). Both women's subordination to the job needs of men and the willingness of older workers to retire early is now diminishing.

Austria too has been highly successful in holding down unemployment, even in the post-shock periods, but its main instruments have been fiscal, incomes, and social policies, not ALMP. Austria gets good returns on the ALMP money it spends, however (see Katzenstein 1984:42; OECD 1967a). Social partnership sets the context for all policies.

Because our qualitative rankings are based both on resource commitment and successful implementation, we have placed Austria in the middle of the pack to balance low effort against high success for the limited effort sustained. Much of Austria's success on the labor supply side comes from its commitment to vocational training in the educational system. Like Germany and Switzerland, Austria integrates school and work through an extensive apprenticeship system. Apprenticeship is a grey area in the measurement of ALMP that has yet to be sorted out by analysts of labor-market policy.

Medium-ranking *Netherlands* had an outstanding performance during 1950-74, almost matching the low average unemployment of Sweden and Japan. Its rank of five reflects the decreasing success of all its policies since the early 1970s. Established just after World War II, its ALMP has been run by a strong General Directorate for Manpower, advised by tripartite local commissions. Success was apparent in placement, regional job creation, apprenticeship programs, and a modest vocational training effort, with some job creation in public service. Concepts, programs, and expenditures expanded greatly after 1969. But ALMP grew increasingly expensive because of the extensive use of government employment as a last resort for the handicapped and unemployed, with full public-employee status and good pay in industrial production centers and the public services. ALMP proved unable to combine effectively with other public policies to prevent unemployment from rising to 12 percent in 1983. Increasing tension and rigidity marked the positions between the social partners (business and labor).

The bottom three—France, the United States, and the United Kingdom—made no major commitment to ALMP until the 1960s and either vacillated in their budgets and policies or saw ALMP as incidental. The early *French* focus on industrial policy, modernization, and restructuring for the most part did not include ALMP. It can be argued that the French planners have hardly distinguished between industrial and labor-market policies. For instance, when they anticipate a plant shutdown in one area, they often try to locate new enterprises in the area through selective credit allocation and other financial instruments (Cohen 1977). In any case, while ALMP was very weak before the events of 1968, it expanded in the early 1970s, emphasizing job placement and training, with some success. The labor-market board expanded rapidly both as a placement service and a coordinator of ALMP.

In the years of "liberal" austerity (1976-81) aimed at industrial redeployment, unemployment was viewed as a secondary problem; ALMP was cut back as unemployment rose. Training programs continued (apprenticeships and on-the-job training as well as subsidies to firms to hire youth). Some studies showed that unemployment was not thereby reduced; instead employers benefited from cheap temporary labor and deferred permanent hiring (Mouriaux and Mouriaux 1984:157). The larger the firm, the greater the windfall—a pattern common to several countries (Haveman 1982; Casey and Bruche 1985:47). In 1981, the new Socialist government, responding to rising unemployment, began substantial expansion of ALMP: it strengthened the labor-market board (1,500 new staff jobs), created a new ministry for occupational training, set up local job-creation programs run by tripartite local committees (250 by 1982), and expanded subsidies to firms for hiring the hard-to-employ. The Mitterrand/Mauroy government also pushed for worksharing. Although there have been scattered successes (Mouriaux and Mouriaux 1984), the net effect is in doubt. Clearly, ALMP was not able to counter other Socialist policies in 1981 and 1982 that increased the unemployment rate—reflationary measures in the face of austerity measures adopted by France's trading partners, increased minimum wages and social spending, nationalizations that increased managerial uncertainty and alienated business and banking circles. Reversals in these policies came too late to repair either the economic or political damage. Although France fits our hypotheses before Mitterrand, we shall see that it is an exception across all policy areas and measures of policy impact in the early 1980s.

The *United States* had no ALMP during 1946-62; in fact, a rather active employment service was gutted after World War II and became a passive agency for employer and veteran needs, by the 1980s accounting for less than 10 percent of new hires. From 1962 to 1982 the United States adopted a moderate range of job-training and job-creation policies, with some success. From a very limited base, funding climbed through the Johnson, Nixon, Ford, and Carter administrations. With minor fluctuations, annual federal outlays in employment and training programs moved from less than one tenth of one percent of GNP in 1950-64 to a peak of .52 percent in 1978 and 1979. Under President Reagan's assault on civilian public spending for the nonaged, outlays had dropped to .18 percent by 1983 (Wilensky 1985:17). For any one type of program, however, funding tended to be unsteady, coordination among programs weak, and political contention intense. With some exceptions and in contrast to European practice, the accent was more on short-term formal evaluation and experimentation than on program implementation, administration, intensity, and outreach (Haveman and Saks 1985:26; Wilensky 1985, 1983; Aaron 1978). Performance reflects the lack of consensus on the importance of unemployment reduction and the lack of structures for linking ALMP to other policies.

The *United Kingdom* shows a stop-and-go pattern as erratic as that of the United States. ALMP started in the mid-1960s, expanded in the mid-1970s—under Labour governments—and were cut back in 1979-80 by the Thatcher government. The 1973 Education and

Training Act strengthened industrial training grants and exemptions and created a tripartite Manpower Services Commission (MSC) to run public employment and training and plan a long-term manpower policy. Funding expanded for a wide range of programs. Despite initial cutbacks in ALMP by the Conservatives (adult employment subsidies, for example, were cut 50-75 percent), the role of the MSC has continued to grow in response to dramatic increases in unemployment (Moon 1984:32). Since 1980 the Thatcher government has expanded ALMP to a level now exceeding that of the last Labour government; the main policy instrument has been the Youth Training Scheme (Casey and Bruche 1985:56; McArthur and McGregor 1986).

The big problem for the United Kingdom has been disjunction between ALMP and other policies such as fiscal and monetary measures to fight inflation and defend sterling (Moon 1984:34). Unemployment rose from 2.6 percent in 1970 to 12.2 percent in 1982. ALMP has doubtless created some jobs and trained workers, but unemployment remains very high. Despite the recent ALMP expansion, the success of ongoing industrial and employment-adjustment efforts remains very much in doubt.*

INDUSTRIAL POLICY

The goals of industrial policy, according to both advocates and critics, are even more numerous than those of ALMP. Consider this list: improvement of market characteristics by encouraging competition, preventing monopoly, or promoting mergers; stimulation of innovation; smoothing of structural adaptation of labor or capital to changing conditions; restructuring of international

---

*Critics of "European" labor-market policies argue that comparisons of the unemployment rates of the United States and, say, those of Sweden, Austria, or Germany are misleading because they ignore the superior job-creation record of the United States, at least since 1976. For a discussion of the ambiguity of growth in rates of employment (vs. unemployment) as a measure of economic performance, see Appendix B. It shows why there is no consensus on this issue, while there *is* general agreement that the combination of low unemployment, low inflation, and high persistent, real growth is desirable.

economic relations via trade creation and trade diversion—and more*
(Adams and Klein, eds. 1983:16-17, 51-53). They all add up to
improving national growth and competitiveness, without which none
of the specific goals is likely to be achieved.

Perhaps the best single measure for evaluating the success of the
industrial policy package is sustained growth. Table 3 therefore aligns

Table 3

INDUSTRIAL POLICY:
QUALITATIVE RANK AND ECONOMIC GROWTH

Summary Ranking of Successful Implementation Inferred from Literature Cited	Average Annual Growth in Real GDP per Capita[a] (Percent and Rank)		
	1950-74	1975-79	1980-84
1. Japan	8.0%(H)	3.8%(H)	3.3%(H)
2. France	4.2(HM)	2.6(H)	0.6(L)
3. West Germany	4.7(H)	2.6(H)	1.0(M)
4. Austria	4.6(H)	2.4(H)	1.6(M+)
5. Sweden	3.2(ML)	0.2(L)	1.4(M)
6. Netherlands	3.8(M)	1.6(L)	-0.3(L)
7. United Kingdom	2.3(L)	1.9(M)	0.5(L)
8. United States	2.4(L)	2.8(H)	0.9(ML)
Average for nineteen rich democracies	3.7	1.9	1.3

[a]For sources, see Appendix B.

*The "more" is reflected in another list of goals for industrial policy as-
sembled by the Trilateral Commission: long-run efficiency—i.e., a dynamic
economy; the freedom and health of the market system; social aims such as a
good environment, job security, and full employment; economic and strategic
security; international cooperation (Pinder et al. 1979:38-39, 68).

real (inflation-adjusted) annual growth in GDP per capita for the three postwar periods next to our qualitative ranks. This growth measure is generally considered a good clue to increases in the standard of living. The qualitative rankings of success match the growth rates quite well in the 1950-74 period, with the most active countries showing the best growth rates and the least committed countries showing the poorest growth. After the two oil shocks, three exceptions stand out among the sixteen post-1974 entries in Table 3: Sweden in 1975-79 is perhaps too low in growth for its medium qualitative rank, although it regains a medium performance after 1979; in 1980-84 France is much too low in growth for its high qualitative rank; and the United States in 1975-79 is much too high in growth for its low rank (although the cost was high inflation and unemployment). Among the several explanations for these discrepancies, one is most persuasive. By any measure of vulnerability to the oil shocks, Sweden is most vulnerable, and the United States, least. For instance, among nineteen rich democracies in 1970, Sweden was third in its dependence on oil (83 percent of its total energy consumption) and seventeenth in its domestic energy production (energy production as a percentage of energy consumption). The United States was the mirror image: nineteenth in oil dependence (41 percent of total energy consumption) and third in domestic energy production (91 percent of consumption); see Appendix B.* France, although medium in its vulnerability to oil shocks, managed a strong performance in 1975-79 but (for the reasons discussed above) fell sharply in growth during the last period. The combination of mounting tensions between government and industry and the Mitterrand reflation of the early 1980s were fatal for economic performance.

Again Appendix A presents a description and chronology of policies by country. A brief characterization of degrees of national

---

*In addition, the United States ranks high in post-shock growth with the help of a big decline in the price of its exports from 1973 to 1980—a depreciation of the dollar, which, together with relatively slow rises in wages and profits, more than offset the slower growth in U.S. manufacturing productivity compared to its competitors (Lawrence 1984:50, 95-96). After 1980, the situation reversed.

commitment and success may help. What Sweden is to ALMP, *Japan* is to industrial policy: the standout case of a highly organized and centralized policy, embracing a wide range of subsidies and financial instruments, highly successful in industrial development and in continuous and speedy economic adjustment throughout the postwar period (Johnson 1982, 1984; Yamamura 1982; Hosomi and Okumura 1982; Zysman and Tyson 1984; Magaziner and Reich 1982). Currently Japan's advanced technology industries remain highly competitive. Some problems may be developing due to over-production resulting from past investment subsidies in a protected market—in industries such as shipbuilding, steel, and aluminum refining (Yamamura 1982:92). Ironically, industrial policy is com-plicated by trade conflicts rooted in the great success of past policy. If past is prologue, however, Japan will use its strong bureaucratic apparatus in government and industry to manage an orderly decline of its losers.

France, the runner-up in effort and to a lesser extent in per-formance, had a successful industrial policy from the late 1940s into the 1970s. Its celebrated indicative planning, established after the war, developed into a strong industrial policy, especially after 1958 under Charles deGaulle. As in Japan, the system was based on a powerful and effective state bureaucracy, close government-business relations, and the exclusion of labor from major policymaking (although tripartite advisory committees abound). Government inter-vention includes nationalization, regulation, and—most important—control of financial instruments for selective credit allocation. Signs of success: a rapid move from agriculture to industry, the building of a modern industrial structure (including the necessary infrastructure) with large consolidated firms; good real growth sustained through three decades. Troubles are also obvious: some French industries in the 1980s are losing to international competition (for example, autos and computers); industrial conflict continues at a high level; restructuring efforts are often reactive on a grand scale (big subsidies to textiles, steel, and shipbuilding); and planners are slow to abandon large, complicated prestige projects. Civilian R & D—small compared to West Germany's and Japan's—is focused on nuclear energy, aircraft, and computers (Magaziner and Reich 1982:278-79, 285).

West Germany's industrial policy can be described as adaptive, positive, and largely informal; it is less comprehensive than that of Japan or France. After the war the Adenauer government, with Ludwig Erhard as Minister of Economics, embraced a free-market ideology, with the Bundesbank accenting tight money and the government later emphasizing Keynesian demand management and an expansive welfare state. With appropriate tradeoffs—ALMP, job protection, codetermination, and works councils—unions accepted wage moderation, industrial peace, and the competition of immigrant labor.

Since 1966, when the Social Democratic Party (SPD) entered the government as part of "the Grand Coalition," an industrial policy has developed with new tripartite structures, including business, banks, government, and labor. The Grand Coalition laid the consensus and information-gathering base for an effective industrial policy. Generally—and with an increasing number of recent exceptions—the federal government has rejected those structural policies that aim to preserve the status quo (Wagenhals 1983). In 1969 legislation for regional investment subsidies was adopted; from 1972 into the 1980s a diversified industrial policy was implemented by the new Ministry of Technology (for growth industries), the Ministry of Economics (for declining industries), and the *Länder* with special links to para-state banks (for strong regional development policies) (Curzon Price 1981:5, 50-51; Magaziner and Reich 1982:262, 279-82, 312). Since 1969 West Germany has successfully managed sectoral decline and adjustment, and an industrial policy has clearly helped to improve productivity and modernization in the high-technology industries (Wagenhals 1983:256-57).

Although West Germany has no directing agency like Japan's MITI and major decisions and implementation remain in private hands, the government plays an important role in promoting both innovations and consensus. However, conflict between *Sozialpolitik* and neoliberal ideologies and groups has increased since the mid-1970s. It is unclear whether West Germany is keeping up with Japan and the United States in advanced technology, unemployment has soared, workers are restive, and unions express frustration with their secondary role in the consensus. Some unions are reviewing their previous positive posture regarding technological change.

In *Austria* industrial policy is embedded in a consensual, tripartite negotiating process which has guided industrial decisions since World War II; it evolved from a social partnership between unions and employers with government support and participation but not necessarily direct leadership. Because two thirds of the fifty largest corporations are nationalized and because the government has a central position in financial markets, the state is in a strong position to guide economic development—but not in the dirigiste sense as in France and Japan. The Austrian government proclaims an activist industrial policy but is constrained by its dedication to consensus (Katzenstein 1984). Broad "Austro-Keynesian" policies have predominated, as opposed to specific sectoral policies.

Government policies in support of corporatist bargaining arrangements, with strong commitment to an incomes policy, job protection, price surveillance, and expansive social policies, have yielded consistently high growth with low unemployment and low inflation throughout the postwar period. Industrial policy—small-step, reactive, flexible—has been the dessert in this menu of policies. Although Austria, like the rest of our eight countries, has been falling short of its industrial policy goals since the mid-1970s, there are signs of further adaptation. Its Keynesian strategy is being reoriented toward structural readjustment based on a fair sharing of transition costs, skill upgrading, regional technology centers for small and medium-sized firms, and experiments with regional consortia, including heads of factory councils, chambers of industry and labor, local mayors, and parliamentary representatives in state and nation. The government is playing an increasingly direct role (Katzenstein 1984, 1985; Sabel 1984).

Like Austria, *Sweden* has not developed a coherent active industrial policy in the usual sense. What it has done is a product of larger social and economic strategies devised and implemented through corporatist bargaining arrangements. Unlike Austria, Sweden's sustained high growth in the pre-shock period was not matched in the first post-shock period (in fact, average annual real growth per capita in 1975-79 is the lowest in Table 3). After the second shock, however, Sweden regained its modest growth record.

A de facto industrial policy is implicit in the Rehn/Meidner model, which was discussed and adopted by the Swedish labor movement and the Social Democratic Party in the early 1950s. It consisted of three main themes (compare Scharpf 1983; Martin 1979; Wilensky 1985):

(1) The labor movement should adopt a policy of "wage solidarity" that (a) reduces differentials between skilled and unskilled, (b) provides equal pay for equal work regardless of differences in ability to pay by region and sector. Less profitable firms would thereby be forced to become more efficient or shut down and workers would be displaced.

(2) The government should not try to eliminate all unemployment through Keynesian management of aggregate demand (too inflationary).

(3) The unemployment resulting from (1) and (2) should be countered by an active labor market policy—commitment to placement and counseling services linked to mobility incentives (to encourage mobility from weak to strong regions and sectors) and an expansion of training and retraining opportunities.

This strategy of squeezing out noncompetitive firms, favoring more productive firms, and promoting mobility combined with centralized collective bargaining adds up to a kind of industrial policy since it aims in part to force competitiveness and continually restructure industry.

From 1970 to 1982 Sweden pursued more typically interventionist industrial policies to save jobs and investments in declining industries such as steel and shipbuilding and/or restore their competitiveness. Industrial policy was at first reactive and ad hoc (Belfrage and Molleryd 1984:177; Scharpf 1981:30). In the late 1970s the government decided to give large capital grants to selected companies; these were described as both industrial policy (for structural adaptation) and ALMP (for job protection and creation). But employment goals seemed to take precedence over industrial policy goals (Henning 1984:197-205). The result was a public accustomed to job and training opportunities and horrified at an unemployment rate that might approach 4 percent. In general, the prior success of the Rehn/Meidner model and the need for consensus make it hard to develop a new strategy for economic growth and adjustment in the cold economic climate of the past decade. Since 1982, however, reactive policies have been replaced by more pro-active and successful efforts: the government has reduced subsidies to declining industries, expanded support for R & D, and promoted the rapid introduction of advanced technology. By the mid-1980s the Swedish economy was improving in a surge of export-led growth.

The Netherlands, United Kingdom, and United States have intermittently undertaken only limited measures with even more limited success. In the reconstruction years, 1945-50, the *Netherlands* had an effective industrial policy based on tripartite agreement. This policy contributed to the great success of reconstruction and the subsequent "economic miracle" of the 1950s and 1960s. Except for a regional development policy and ad hoc measures to support such weak industries as shipbuilding, textiles, and mining, and the promotion in the 1970s of a few international high-tech ventures (e.g., aircraft and satellites), the Netherlands has not had an organized industrial policy since the early 1950s (Wolinetz 1983; Katzenstein 1985). Dramatic economic growth in the 1950s and 1960s and an abundance of natural gas in the 1970s have deferred the discussion of an active industrial policy. The government also has few levers over finance and industrial capital (Wolinetz 1985:49). Finally, shifts in structures for bargaining in the 1970s—employer associations more tough and centralized, union federations more decentralized, smaller unions amalgamating and resisting central federation controls—have threatened the corporatist consensus. In these circumstances the policy focus has been on general measures for growth, employment, and redistribution rather than on industrial structure.

In the 1980s Dutch elites have revived discussion of a focused industrial policy; they see it as led by an expert commission, not by the tripartite Social and Economic Council or the bipartite Foundation of Labor. Despite some weakening of corporatist struc-tures, they remain in place, a channel for dialogue (Wolinetz 1983). There is no doubt, however, that the consensus-making machine of the earlier period is now moving in low gear—like the Dutch economy in the first half of the 1980s.

The *United Kingdom* has tried all sorts of policies, depending on the political swings between Labour and Tory governments and rather sharp economic fluctuations. As with British incomes policies, any short-term successes are cut short by these political and economic swings. Despite its powerful permanent bureaucracy, the United Kingdom evidences little continuity of policy and action in this area. With few exceptions tripartite, government-led attempts at planning have so far failed to restructure and rejuvenate British industry. The National Economic Development Corporation, established in 1961, spawned many "little Neddies" for specific sectors (Curzon Price 1981:57); a short-lived National Plan in the mid-1960s was followed by a tripartite Industrial Reorganization Corporation in 1967-70 to promote mergers and rationalization (Pinder et al. 1979:34). In the 1970s industrial policy was largely reduced to subsidies for declining industries (e.g., troubled firms like British Leyland) and unselective regional policies. (For recent efforts to channel capital to new high-tech projects—e.g., the Microelectronic Industry Support Scheme—see Appendix A.)

The pattern of policy failure is rooted in the lack of mechanisms for achieving consensus and agreement among major economic power blocs; a strong but fragmented and decentralized labor movement; employers, equally fragmented, who insist on autonomy except when they are failing; and a powerful financial community oriented toward international investments. No one is strong enough to impose the costs of adjustment on others, nor are labor and management cohesive enough to forge consensus on sharing costs.

To the extent that the *U.S.* government has had "industrial policies," they have been macroeconomic (fiscal and monetary), anti-trust (to prevent major decreases in domestic competition), national security (defense spending, military and space R & D, including funding and guidance of R & D via direct procurement as in aviation, computers, and semiconductors), or reactive (trade restrictions such as tariffs, quotas, "Orderly Marketing Agreements," trigger prices for troubled sectors, and occasional bailouts for troubled firms such as Chrysler and Lockheed).

Some states in the United States, especially in recent years, have adopted innovative policies that may have promoted new investment and, to some extent, the restructuring of industry. Typically, however, state policies are of the "beggar-thy-neighbor" variety, as when states compete for new plants with tax and land subsidies. Such policies are unlikely to increase the total GNP of the

United States. Even the most innovative state policies do not form part of a coherent national industrial policy. Unconnected to national efforts and the programs of other states, frequently becoming part of a zero-sum game, state-level policy remains marginal to our definition of industrial policy (see above, pp. 3 and 6).

In historical perspective, this absence of a positive industrial policy since World War II is puzzling, for the United States pioneered one of the most successful coordinated government-civilian sector development policies in the history of modern nations—the promotion of agriculture. In the nineteenth century, aside from giving land grants to farmers, the federal government established a huge network of land-grant colleges and agricultural experiment stations, combining basic and applied research and teaching with outreach to farmers through agricultural extension services and widespread participation by farm organizations. As a result of more than a century of this sectoral industrial policy, about 3 percent of the labor force produces an agricultural surplus that by 1973 accounted for 25 percent of total American exports and even during the agricultural depression of the 1980s still accounted for about 18 percent (figures for 1982-84). Begun in the heyday of entrepreneurial capitalism, these productivity-enhancing programs have continued to expand in the age of the welfare state. Yet today, except for agriculture and defense, the United States has backed away from any attempt to manage structural change and in the 1980s is relying on two contradictory strategies: deregulation along with a loose fiscal policy in the hope of indirectly increasing investment, productivity, and growth; and continuing trade restrictions in the hope of slowing down the collapse of losing industries.

INCOMES POLICY

Under different economic circumstances governments that directly intervene to induce wage restraint have emphasized different goals—a reduction of inflation or unemployment or both, preventing deterioration in the terms of trade, and so on. Moreover, policymakers have not always been clear on whether they aim to restrain money wages or real wages, wage rates or earnings, or whether they have their eye on the long run or the short. It is apparent that where the aim is temporary—e.g., wage and price controls in a crisis—the effect is also temporary because everyone goes for catch-up increases when controls are off. Thus we shall again concentrate on persistent policies and long-term aggregate effects. This time we supplement qualitative rankings with both inflation rates and unemployment rates because they are equally important clues to the overriding goal of incomes policies—to control wage-push inflation without incurring great costs in unemployment. (See Table 4.) The alternative, rejected by the advocates of incomes policy, is to run a high unemployment rate or a general recession to wring out inflation.

The match of each component with the qualitative rankings of success is not as good as when we equally weight our ratings for both inflation and unemployment. (For the combined ranks in Table 4, low is best.) Of three policy clusters, incomes policies appear to be most ambiguous in their effects in these eight countries.*

The top three countries in Table 4 either had consistent policies of wage restraint and consistent success for almost all of the postwar period (Austria, West Germany) or a persistent de facto incomes policy with similar success (Sweden). (For details, see Appendix A.) *Austria* has had a continuous incomes policy from 1947 to the present, with low wage drift and (like West Germany and Sweden) few strikes. The government functions as a guide to the social partners, making wage restraint palatable by providing strong social policies, an ALMP, job protection, and price surveillance, combined with macroeconomic policies aimed at economic growth (Addison 1981:211ff.). Austria avoided the wage explosions of the late 1960s and early 1970s—common in most rich democracies—partly because its incomes policy did not lead to real wage declines (Flanagan, Soskice, and Ulman 1983:43). Rank-and-file revolt has been minimized through the combination of centralized authority in the Austrian Trade Union Federation (ÖGB), decentralized local

---

*Because incomes policies did not fully take hold until the 1960s, the use of 1950-74 for inferring effects might be misleading. But a correlation matrix for nineteen rich countries shows that average rates of inflation by different periods are highly correlated (e.g., inflation 1950-74 by inflation 1961-74 equals .85). Correlations of unemployment rates by period are similarly strong (e.g., average unemployment 1950-74 by average unemployment 1960-74 equals .89).

Table 4

INCOMES POLICY: QUALITATIVE RANK, INFLATION, AND UNEMPLOYMENT

Summary Ranking of Successful Implementation of Incomes Policy Inferred from Literature Cited	Average Annual Inflation Rates[a] (Percent and Rank)			Average Annual Unemployment Rates[a] (Percent and Rank)			Combined Ranks: Inflation & Unemployment		
	1950-74	1975-79	1980-84	1950-74	1975-79	1980-84	1950-74	1975-79	1980-84
1. Austria	5.3%(M)	5.7%(L)	5.3%(LM)	2.2%(L)	1.8%(L)	3.2%(L)	ML	L	L
2. West Germany	3.8(L)	4.4(L)	3.7(L)	2.6(M)	3.6(M)	6.3(M)	LM	LM	LM
3. Sweden	5.1(M)	13.3(M)	9.5(M)	1.7(L)	1.9(L)	2.8(L)	LM	LM	ML
4. Japan	5.7(H)	5.9(L)	2.0(L)	1.7(L)	1.9(L)	2.4(L)	M	L	L
5. Netherlands	5.0(M)	7.9(L)	4.3(L)	1.8(L)	4.0(M)	10.7(H)	LM	ML	M
6. France	5.8(H)	10.4(M)	10.7(H)	2.4(ML)	4.6(MH)	7.9(M)	M	M	HM
7. United Kingdom	5.0(M)	16.4(H)	9.6(M)	2.7(M)	4.5(MH)	9.5(H)	M	HM	HM
8. United States	3.2(L)	6.9(L)	6.7(LM)	5.2(H)	6.8(H)	8.2(M)	M	M	LM
Average for nineteen rich countries	5.0	12.2	8.2	2.9	3.9	6.8			

[a]For sources, see Appendix B.

negotiations, and the integration of shop stewards into the tightly linked network of Socialist Party and labor organizations (Flanagan, Soskice, and Ulman 1983: 80; Katzenstein 1984; Houska 1985). Although white-collar unions have recently become restive, national bargaining is still intact.

West Germany has had continuous incomes policies, formal or informal, since the early 1950s. Unions have shown wage restraint through most of the postwar period, although incomes policy played only a modest role relative to monetary policy, social policy, co-determination, and social partnership (A. Wilson 1982:55; Flanagan, Soskice, and Ulman 1983:284-94).

Government and Bundesbank recommendations and wage guidelines have transformed collective bargaining into a forge for shaping an incomes policy. Especially during the decade of "Concerted Action," 1966-77, the unions explicitly traded off wage restraint for a government commitment to full employment and institutional equality (Flanagan, Soskice, and Ulman 1983:280). Concerted Action provided a tripartite forum for discussions of policy interdependence (e.g., linking wages to economic growth and job protection), as well as government input on other issues. It also led to rank-and-file rebellion and big wage increases in 1969 and 1973 (Flanagan, Soskice, and Ulman 1983:286-88). For most of the 1970s and early 1980s, however, West German collective-bargaining agreements continued to evidence wage restraint (A. Wilson 1982:54). Even in 1984 the largest postwar strike yielded only modest gains in the face of high unemployment. One of the strains on the system has been the failure to directly integrate monetary and fiscal policies into wage- and price-setting (Flanagan, Soskice, and Ulman 1983:285)—reflecting the autonomy and power of the Bundesbank as well as the centralization and superior discipline of the employers' federation (BDA). On balance, though, incomes policy gets a share of credit for West Germany's relatively good long-term performance on prices and unemployment.

What might be called a de facto incomes policy was sustained by *Sweden* throughout the postwar period. In a quite centralized collective bargaining system labor and management negotiate, but the government plays a strong role, offering inducements to wage restraint. LO (the largest union federation) and SAF (an almost all-encompassing employers' federation) are both highly centralized, powerful, and quite disciplined. Labor has political strength, an economywide perspective, and a solidaristic (egalitarian) wage policy; all parties see a close relation between wage levels, labor-market and social policy, industrial policy, and macroeconomic policy. (See section on ALMP above.) Even for most of the difficult years of 1970-85 wages remained in line with government policy (Katzenstein 1985:50-51). During the entire postwar period, among these eight countries Sweden rates medium on inflation and ties Japan for the best unemployment record.

From 1970 to 1985 there was increasing strain on the Swedish system. The standard economic difficulties, exacerbated by Sweden's unusual vulnerability to the oil shocks, were accompanied by episodes of worker discontent, wage drift, and white-collar union opposition to LO's egalitarian wage policy (Martin 1984:248-346). More government involvement in the bargaining process met with mixed success in wage restraint. From 1982 to 1985 there was a small shift toward decentralization of collective bargaining and a weakening of incomes policy. PTK (salaried unions in the private sector) broke away from national wage agreements in 1982, the metal workers in 1983. But PTK and LO agreed to coordinate again with SAF in 1984, and the government continues as an active partner orchestrating tradeoffs (e.g., in 1985 an agreement to cut inflation to 3 percent while wages rose 5 percent; in 1984 the establishment of investment funds, a move toward labor co-ownership, in part as a tradeoff for wage restraint) (Wilensky interviews). In general, Sweden's corporatist democracy has so far proven quite resilient (see Wilensky 1976; Flanagan, Soskice, and Ulman 1983; Katzenstein 1985).

Japan has fought inflation mainly through fiscal and monetary policy with occasional price controls; wage moderation occurs in the context of company-dominated industrial relations, enterprise unionism, and tight government-industry interaction. Both sides know that the government can and will intervene if necessary. Wage raises have generally been held to the level of productivity increases; wage-push inflation has for the most part been avoided. The government occasionally jawbones, meeting with labor leaders prior to the traditional spring negotiations to communicate its inflation goals. This has no force of law but is an effective form of pressure:

In short, Japan has no formal wage policy. It does, however, have a social contract buttressed by the structure of its industrial relations that invokes a kind of soft incomes policy (Nanto 1982: 42; compare Levine 1983).

When the government has wanted wage restraint, it has generally and informally secured it, especially after the wage explosion of 1974. After the oil shocks a new tripartite joint consultation machinery was established, and both unemployment and inflation have been relatively low.

The Netherlands had an active incomes policy throughout the postwar period. The structure of wage bargaining assures government participation through the Board of Government Mediators. Despite the division of confessional-political blocs in both the labor movement and the party system, a tripartite postwar social partnership has underpinned government efforts at wage restraint. In the past two decades, a tendency toward government-imposed wage moderation developed from the tripartite framework and has been tacitly accepted by organized labor and industry.

The fair to good medium performance of the Netherlands in Table 4 is explained by alternating success and failure. Generally incomes policy was very successful until 1963; then the pressures of full employment, worker dissatisfaction with low wages (especially in such profitable industries as natural gas), and increasing economic diversification as well as a gradual erosion of "pillarization" undermined social consensus and led to incomes policy failures in 1963-75 (Flanagan, Soskice, and Ulman 1983; Houska 1985).* Wages rose more than productivity and more than wages in other European countries. In the early 1980s the government pursued an uncompensated

---

*Versuiling, literally "columnization" or "pillarization," refers to the separate pillars (*zuilen*) of Dutch society, each indispensable in supporting the national structure. They are the major confessional-political blocs—Calvinist, Roman Catholic, "general," socialist, and at times a latitudinarian Protestant bloc. Each has encompassed a whole array of organizations, including political parties, labor unions, industry groups, schools and universities, health and welfare agencies, radio and television corporations, and sports and leisure associations. Segmented at the bottom, they have been integrated at the top through national accommodations. Although this complex cultural-political system still exists, it is plainly in decline as a structural basis for consensus.

incomes policy, including deflation, high unemployment, and cutbacks in social transfers (Wolinetz 1983:24).

France, the United Kingdom, and the United States have had no
sustained incomes policy; at best they have undertaken intermittent
experiments with limited and always short-term success. (See Appendix A for chronology.) Their middling combined rank on inflation
and unemployment is a product of other forces and policies.

In *France* there was no negotiated incomes policy and no direct
government intervention except in 1964-68 and 1976-78. Long-term
wage restraint is not due to incomes policies but rather to labor
disunity and weakness and employer strength. In the context of close
government-industry relations and a divided, ideologically raucous
labor movement, employers set wages. There was virtually no effective
collective bargaining before 1968. In general, the postwar pattern
has been to grant wage increases when necessary to reduce unrest,
then let inflation reduce gains. Both the strongest labor federation
(the CGT) and the employers' federation (the CNPF) have opposed
any incomes policy.

The *United Kingdom* has experimented with incomes policies
but always for short periods and with short-term impact. The best
results have come with Labour in power and with the cooperation of
the Trades Union Congress (TUC). These attempts have been undermined by economic stagnation and inflation, sterling crises, the
alternation of governments, the weakness of the TUC, and a decentralized industrial relations system with plenty of room for parochial bargaining and wage drift. From 1964 to 1970, continuous,
explicit incomes policies with short-term medium effectiveness were
undermined by political conflict, wage drift, and the decision to
defend the value of the sterling. The result was stalemate between
unions and employers; unions had little incentive for restraint.
From 1974 to 1979 incomes policy had high short-term success;
wage restraint was traded for social and labor legislation. But the
breakdown of the "social contract," with escalating wage demands
and the 1978-79 "winter of discontent," helped bring down the
Labour government and spelled the end of incomes policy. In sum,
during the entire postwar period, the rate of wage inflation was
reduced for brief periods, followed by catch-up increases; the net
effect was an increase in the instability of the inflation rate. (Fallick

and Elliot, eds. 1981:260-61; Flanagan, Soskice, and Ulman 1983; Blank 1978). The Thatcher government opposes incomes policy; wages are held down by deflationary fiscal and monetary policies and direct challenges to union power.

In the *United States* four attempts at organized incomes policies since World War II found only limited and short-lived success primarily because wage decisions are highly dispersed throughout the economy. As of 1979 only 30 percent of private-sector workers were covered by collective bargaining agreements, which are often local and craft-based. The AFL-CIO has no authority to enforce any incomes policy. Although wages were restrained during the 1960s Kennedy "guideposts," a wage explosion followed which led to wage-and-price controls during the Nixon administration. Inflation rose again in 1974 and continued into the early 1980s. Long-term wage and inflation rates have probably been unaffected by these brief attempts (Pencavel 1981; Rees 1979).

Chapter 5

SUMMARY AND INTERPRETATION

Democratic corporatism as a structure for national bargaining among major interest groups under the formal and informal auspices of government fosters strong linkages. Well-organized, centralized labor and professional associations, facing similar employer associations and at least moderately centralized governments, show these policy linkages in three ways. First, their leaders—top union officials, top managers in industry and commerce, politicians and bureaucrats in government—are aware of the interdependence of public policies and their effects. Second, they have developed channels for dialogue and reciprocal influence, both private and public, concerning a wide range of issues and have frequently and flexibly made tradeoffs relevant to the changing economic circumstances they confront. Third, the experts and intellectuals in these bipartite and tripartite bargaining structures give the bargaining process a more "rational-responsible" bias than is common in less corporatist democracies; the linkages of experts and their bosses across functional, regional, and social (ethnic, religious, linguistic, racial) lines foster tradeoffs that reduce conflict and create consensus and thereby make policy implementation more effective.

A variant of democratic corporatism—corporatism without labor—at first glance has less need for tight linkages across all policy areas, less need for tradeoffs counterposing industrial and incomes policies to social and labor-market policies. The main actors from business and government are less attentive to social and labor-market policies of keen interest to labor. Indeed our two cases of this variant, France and Japan, evidence somewhat less policy interdependence in elite perception and action than do Sweden, Austria, and the FRG, and, for most of the postwar period, less interdependence than the Netherlands. Industrial policy dominates the rest.

The least corporatist democracies, the United States and the United Kingdom, as expected, show most policy segmentation and least policy continuity. Because the United States has the most fragmented and decentralized political economy among the eight countries considered, it best illustrates structural barriers to policy linkages. In fact, among the universe of rich democracies, with the possible exception of Switzerland, there is no more decentralized federalism, no greater division of powers, no weaker central government. The dogma of local self-government is enshrined in the U.S. constitution and laws; a federal system divides powers among thousands of counties, townships, municipalities, and other local units. In order to survive, the modern metropolis, which cross-cuts these arbitrary boundaries, is forced to create a staggering number of special district governments, each concentrating on a limited area-wide task, each competing for budget, tax base, or subsidy, all adding to the maze of overlapping and duplicating units. It is free enterprise in government—with every municipality, every district, every state, and every branch of the central government for itself (Wilensky 1965:xviii-xix).

Similarly, the number and organizational structure of U.S. trade associations and labor unions do not permit them to formulate policies that cross-cut industries, functions, and policy domains. In 1980 there were 168 national unions and about 3,200 trade associations—both far more numerous and specialized than their counterparts in Western Europe and Japan. In general, coordinated action by these trade associations is rare, and when it occurs, it is an ad hoc arrangement to cope with specific issues. Thus neither labor federations nor trade associations can be used by the federal government to formulate and implement broad national policy (industrial, occupational health and safety, social security) even if the government were so inclined. They can be used only where policy is narrow and disconnected from broader concerns (cigarette labeling, air traffic control, drug packaging).

When such a system confronts a major problem, its fragmentation is a formidable block to effective action. The recent debate on the need for an industrial policy for the United States is a telling illustration. There is no shortage of pronouncements about the need for such a policy. Such advocates as Felix Rohatyn, Lester Thurow, and Robert Reich express enthusiasm for tripartite commissions or councils; they also argue that industrial restructuring requires that the workers, firms, and communities bearing the burden of change must be compensated by programs of retraining, relocation, and targeted public investment. These debates have led to many meetings among sophisticated business leaders and a few labor leaders. But the representational structures necessary for formulating and implementing a national response is missing; little action occurs. Even where incumbent leaders—not merely outside intellectuals and elder statesmen, but men of power—are aware of the imperatives of policy linkage and try to act, implementation falters, as we have seen in the sorry tale of the Trade Adjustment Assistance Act of 1962.

That policy linkage and continuity foster success in the four areas covered is generally confirmed for these eight countries. By examining the sequence of initiation and expansion of diverse policies since World War II we can conclude that the adoption and expansion of industrial and incomes policies are either accompanied or preceded by the initiation and expansion of active labor-market policies and/or social policies that permit sharing of the burdens and benefits of wage restraint and structural change. Even Japan, a social-policy laggard, has increasing linked ALMP to its economic policies, while France, at first neglecting ALMP, has increasingly linked social policy to industrial policy. By inferring degrees of success and failure from qualitative and quantitative data, we found an interaction of strong corporatism, tight policy linkages, and reasonable success. (Evidence of success is more consistent for industrial policy and ALMP than for incomes policy.) The exceptions can be explained in part by extreme vulnerability to the oil shocks (Sweden's "fair" economic performance in 1975-79) or the attenuation of corporatist bargaining arrangements (the Netherlands's low qualitative ranks for all areas except social policy and its "fair" economic performance in 1975-79; France's move from fair to good and then its fall to poor economic performance in1980-84 under Mitterrand).

If the postwar history of these economic and social policies and their implementation tells us anything, it tells us that structures count. Types of political economies predict the kinds of policies governments adopt; even more, how effectively and persistently policies are implemented. The linkage of major economic and political actors in corporatist bargaining systems facilitates policy linkages; it encourages those tradeoffs that improve economic performance. Channels for talk become channels for consistent action. Thus, compared to the more decentralized and fragmented political economies, where policies are segmented, the corporatist democracies on average and over long periods have an economic edge, even where they are more vulnerable to external shocks. To link industrial or incomes policies to labor-market or social policies is to make the whole policy package more effective.

APPENDIXES

A. CHRONOLOGY BY COUNTRY AND POLICY AREA:
ACTIVE LABOR-MARKET, INDUSTRIAL, AND
INCOMES POLICIES

B. MEASURES OF ECONOMIC PERFORMANCE AND
ENERGY DEPENDENCE

CHRONOLOGY BY COUNTRY AND POLICY AREA: ACTIVE LABOR-MARKET, INDUSTRIAL, AND INCOMES POLICIES

For researchers interested in policy trajectories and interaction and for readers who wish to check for themselves our judgments regarding the initiation, expansion, continuity, and effectiveness of policies in each of three areas, in this appendix we reproduce a summary chronology of events and sources.

ACTIVE LABOR-MARKET POLICY

SWEDEN (1), HIGH SUCCESS

Summary comments. Since the late 1950s, Sweden has made the most extensive use of ALMP of the eight observed countries. ALMP has been emphasized over incomes or industrial policy as a central component of the Rehn/Meidner model, which has guided government economic policy since 1957. Expenditures have increased steadily since 1957; unemployment has been kept low even in the worst of economic times. Policies have been implemented by tripartite boards. The size and sophistication of the programs are unrivaled. Investment stabilization funds help maintain full employment through business cycle swings.

Key dates and events

1948-57: ALMP expenditures are small—0.3% of GNP (Henning: 194).

1957-84: Steady rise in expenditures to 2.4% of GNP in 1984 (Rehn: 73); the largest share of this increase is for the demand side (job creation), a smaller share for supply (job training), which has been growing, and the smallest for matching (job search, moving). By 1982, 53.2% for the demand side, 37.9% for the supply side, and 8.9% for matching (Henning: 198).

1957-60: ALMP is implemented as part of the LO's (blue-collar labor federation) Rehn/Meidner model and administered by the tripartite National Labor Market Board and twenty-four county boards, which have broad authority to choose among policy mixes (demand, supply, matching) (Rehn: 69-70). ALMP was conceived as the key to full employment and a cushion for economic adjustment, competitiveness, and growth. In a competitive environment, productive firms survive, others fail, and ALMP provides the necessary labor-market mobility and flexibility.

1965: Beginning of a focus on regional investment, especially in the north, in response to complaints that everyone has had to move south (Rehn: 78-79).

1970: Regional investment subsidies are tied to workforce increases; big increase in size of the Employment Service begins in 1970; ALMP job training and creation hold steady at high levels throughout the 1970s.

Late 1970s: Large capital grants to selected companies to reduce unemployment can be seen primarily as ALMP rather than industrial policy (Henning: 197); people are more reluctant to move now.

1976-84: In spite of a 20% decline in industrial employment, unemployment stays low due to ALMP and an expansion of the public sector (Rehn: 83).

References: Henning (1984); Katzenstein (1985); Rehn (1985); Scharpf (1981, 1983).

WEST GERMANY (2), HIGH SUCCESS

Summary comments. ALMP has been in place in West Germany throughout the postwar period, with a focus on skilled training programs and job creation (especially since 1969). Policies have been directed by the union-oriented Bundesanstalt für Arbeit (BAA; in the Ministry of Labor), with considerable success.

Key dates and events

1944-60: Training funds are limited during reconstruction.

1949-52: Big increase in job-creation programs, which then declines as unemployment declines. Employment Creation Act (1950) is passed to provide for low-interest loans to business.

1952: Labor Exchange Law enacted: the Bundesanstalt für Arbeitslosenversicherung and Arbeitsvermittlung (BAVAV) is established (becomes BAA in 1969) in the Ministry of Labor to direct labor-market policies. Led by a tripartite executive board, BAVAV is given monopoly power over job placement and grows into a large, powerful agency with a high level of penetration in the labor market.

1952-60: Limited training funds available for workers on public assistance and displaced workers.

1960-66: Training expenditures double as economy grows.

1967: BAVAV expands training programs, which now include advanced training and financial support for individuals and institutions.

1969: Labor Promotion Law (AFG) is passed, signaling a big expansion of ALMP. Under this law the BAVAV becomes the BAA, and the legal right of workers to training is established. Included in this expansion are funds for job training (big increases for training and retraining, especially advanced training), job creation (big increases in pure job creation and short-time work supports), and placement (successful and extensive services are continued). For enhanced job security, the Protection against Dismissal Act is passed.

1969-74: The above activities are all expanded under AFG.

1975-77: Big cutbacks in job training and a shift away from advanced training and retraining to lower skilled training for the unemployed.

1976-84: Shift in emphasis from training to job creation, as the latter becomes the chosen ALMP. Emphasis peaks in 1975 and 1979, followed by decline. Employers then emphasize more flexible deployment of labor, such as intrafirm mobility and flexitime (Sengenberger: 339).

1979: New job creation programs: social service, wage subsidy, grants for R&D in small and medium firms.

1979-81: Training funds increase, including advanced training and retraining, but then decline.

1982-83: Labor Market Consolidation Act is passed for the consolidation of a more limited ALMP. Placement services continue through the cutbacks, their position protected by the inclusion of employers, labor, and government (thus no interest-group opposition as in the United States). In its first year in office the new Christian Democrat/Liberal government increases both job creation and training in response to rising unemployment (Casey and Bruche: 56).

References: Casey and Bruche (1985); Janoski (1986: ch. 3); Sengenberger (1984).

JAPAN (3), HIGH SUCCESS

Summary comments. Japan's employment system is enterprise-based: full employment is seen primarily as the responsibility of employers, not government. ALMP is thus limited compared to other countries (OECD 1973b: 23-24), although it has expanded substantially since 1971 and has been a successful complement to an enterprise employment system.

Key dates and events

1947: Employment Security Law establishes the state employment service, the Public Employment Security Offices (PESO), with an extensive network throughout Japan; by 1956, 70% who find jobs do so through PESO (OECD 1973b: 31).

1949: Government is empowered to set up work-relief projects, with 300,000 employed (*ibid.*, p. 32).

1958: Vocational Training Law is enacted to provide integrated programs for training skilled workers (*ibid.*).

1960: Law is passed to provide for the employment of handicapped workers, including training and workshops (*ibid.*, p. 33).

1963: Employment Promotion Measures—counseling and training for unemployed middle-aged and older workers (*ibid.*).

1967: New Vocational Training Law enacted.

1971: National Vocational Training Plan: Five-year plan for training and retraining. ALMP is placed under the jurisdiction of the Ministry of Labor, focused on placement/exchange and vocational training. Placement gets the biggest share of funds: 700 PESO offices by 1971 (OECD 1973b: 34). Training and retraining goes on mainly within firms for employees with lifetime security (p. 131). By 1970 Japan is spending 0.4% of GNP on ALMP (lower than Sweden, the United Kingdom, and West Germany, but higher than the United States; OECD 1974: 53).

1976: Third Basic Employment Measures Plan is enacted for 1976-80, with an emphasis on subsidies for employment adjustment for industrial restructuring (Japan Institute of Labor [JIL] 1979a: 14). For vocational training 421 facilities exist in Japan as of 1979, with 230,000 trainees per year and an average six-month training period (p. 18). Benefits include training allowances and job-seeking and moving expenses; they provide for handicapped, unemployed middle-aged and older workers, and those displaced by economic restructuring (pp. 19-20). Job creation and protection measures provide subsidies to employers who hire and/or train workers from the above groups (p. 20). The Unemployment Insurance System (of thirty years) is replaced by the Employment Insurance System (1974) and the Employment Stabilization Fund System (1977), with the goal of preventing unemployment (e.g., counter-cyclical subsidies for temporary layoffs and training). To support restructuring and maintain full employment, designated industries qualify for substantial employment adjustment grants and training grants. Job creation in 1976-80 includes subsidies to employers to hire middle-aged and older workers, to hire in certain regions and in winter, and to hire workers displaced from projects in regions of high unemployment (pp. 21-22).

References: JIL (1979a); Levine (1983); OECD (1973b, 1974); Shimada (1980).

AUSTRIA (4), MEDIUM SUCCESS

Summary comments. ALMP has not been a major instrument for Austria's full-employment commitment. Demand management, combined with "social partnership" incomes policy, has been most important, with ALMP in a backup role, although one that has grown since 1970. Commitment to economic growth has been combined with commitment to maintain jobs and create new ones (Katzenstein 1985: 77).

Key dates and events

Until 1967: Very limited ALMP, with no central coordinating agency for man-power policy (OECD 1967a: 34). The Public Employment Service (PES) serves mainly as an unemployment service, as workers are cushioned against the market by employment security and unemployment insurance. The PES's most active role is vocational guidance for the young (p. 39).

1970-79: Expenditures for ALMP increase tenfold, to 2% of budget (compared to Sweden's 8%); the full-employment goal is supported by the public sector and nationalized industries, meaning that other labor-market policies can be less extensive and still keep unemployment down (Katzenstein 1984: 41-42). Emphasis on vocational training: full employment for the young through extensive, government-subsidized apprenticeship programs.

1979-85: Continued expansion of ALMP through comprehensive vocational counseling, skill upgrading, and job protection, but much job training remains outdated and is done in small firms without modern technology (Sabel: 356).

References: Katzenstein (1984, 1985); OECD (1967a); Sabel (1984); Soldwedel (1984).

NETHERLANDS (5), MEDIUM SUCCESS

Summary comments. The Netherlands has had ALMP since World War II; government has accepted responsibility for employing the unemployed. Concepts, programs, and expenditures expanded significantly after 1969. Policies have been run by a strong, central employment service, the General Directorate for Manpower (ARBVO, within the Ministry of Social Affairs and Public Health), advised by tripartite local commissions. Extensive social employment has been criticized as an expensive and comfortable shelter for many workers.

Key dates and events

1945: ARBVO directs ALMP and has a monopoly on job placement. Policy instruments include placement and counseling, vocational training, and job creation (public service) for seasonally or structurally unemployed (OECD 1967b: 47).

1951: Regional job-creation policies are implemented for areas of high unem-ployment (*ibid.*, p. 211).

1954-67: Manpower Organization Order provides a legal basis for the expansion of ALMP. Policies evolve to include an extensive placement and counseling system with 90 regional offices (ARBVO-Service); all worker terminations require approval of the regional offices (OECD 1967b: 53). Vocational training expands but remains modest: 25 government centers, with 2,600 total trainees by 1967 (p. 61). An apprenticeship program to train skilled labor expands to include 70,000 apprentices by 1967 (p. 198). Job creation includes effective but limited supplementary employment policy (public works) and effective regional development policies (1959: decentralization of industry to offset overconcentration; 1964: growth centers designated, 56,000 jobs created in 1964-66) (p. 211).

1969: Social Employment Act empowers government to employ handicapped and others unable to find work, in a program run by ARBVO, with jobs provided by municipal governments advised by local tripartite commissions (Haveman 1978: 244). This new law consolidates programs begun after the war. Hired workers are given full public-employee status and decent pay; implementation is to be guided by the notion that work must train and be socially useful (p. 245). The social employment program contains two parts: industrial production centers (60% of those employed) and public services (pp. 243-44).

By 1976: 64,000 workers are employed in the social employment program (up from 8,000 in 1955; Haveman 1978: 247); cost of the program is up to 1% of net national product (p. 249). Problems include adverse incentives and a lack of economic control.

1980s: Center-conservative government cuts back social programs, real wages, ALMP; unemployment is at 12% in 1983.

References: Haveman (1978); OECD (1967b).

FRANCE (6), MEDIUM SUCCESS

Summary comments. Government emphasis is on industrial policy; modernization and restructuring has not for the most part included ALMP. This lack can be seen as one cause for the events of May and June 1968. ALMP expands in the early 1970s, is cut back in the late 1970s, then grows again after 1981 under a Socialist government.

Key dates and events

1963: National Fund for Employment established. Also in existence: an adult vocational training agency (AFPA), which is very small in the late 1960s.

1966: Vocational Training Law enacted and job-training programs reformed. These are the first major ALMP initiatives in response to unemployment as a problem in the early 1960s, following an influx of repatriates from Algeria (Mouriaux and Mouriaux: 151).

1967: National Employment Agency (ANPE) established.

1968: Worker strikes of May and June lead to the Grenelle agreements, which include expansion of job training and training allowances (OECD 1973a: 61).

1969: Inter-Industry Agreement on Employment Security (as a result of the Grenelle agreements) sets up joint labor and management employment committees in each industry at national and regional levels to examine employment trends and facilitate redeployment and retraining as necessary (*ibid.*, p. 13).

1971: Law passed guaranteeing the right of occupational training to workers.

1971-75: ANPE expands rapidly, both for placement services and to coordinate ALMP (*ibid.*, pp. 15, 26). Adult vocational training increases substantially, from 35,000 trainees in 1968 to 600,000 in 1975 (p. 26).

1975: Laws passed for short-time work compensation and subsidies to firms to offset layoffs.

1976: New era of "liberal" austerity begins for industrial redeployment; unemployment is now seen as a secondary problem (Mouriaux and Mouriaux: 153). ANPE survives but becomes inflexible, with training tied to job offers by employers (*ibid.*). Apprenticeships and on-the-job training programs continue, as well as subsidies to firms to hire youth, but studies show that unemployment is not reduced; rather employers benefit from cheap, temporary manpower and defer permanent hiring (p. 157).

1981: New Socialist government responds to rising unemployment of 1976-81 by strengthening ANPE (1,500 new staff jobs) and creating a new ministry for occupational training. Training funds rise by 28%, and rise again in 1983 (Mouriaux and Mouriaux: 159-60). Local job-creation programs are set up and run by tripartite local committees. By 1982, 250 of these local committees are in existence; they are controversial but often helpful in specific employment zones (p. 163).

1982: Subsidies to firms expand for hiring youth, women, and older workers. Mitterrand/Mauroy government pushes for work-sharing and moves toward a thirty-five-hour week to spread around both work and pay.

References: Mouriaux and Mouriaux (1984); OECD (1973a).

UNITED STATES (7), MEDIUM SUCCESS

Summary comments. The United States had no ALMP to speak of from 1946 to 1962. From 1962 to 1982, a moderate range of job-training and job-creation policies was implemented; these were largely decimated in the Reagan budget cuts.

Key dates and events

1946-60: The active national employment service (USES) is gutted after the war and becomes a passive organization for employer and veteran needs.

1960-69: USES expenditures triple, but placements decline from 15 million in 1960 to 3 million in 1974; funds are cut after 1970.

1962: Manpower and Development Training Act provides the first training programs targeted at blue-collar workers displaced by automation.

1964: Economic Opportunity Act sets up the Job Corps and other programs for the hard-core unemployed. New Careers program is established for technical training.

1965: Emphasis shifts toward blacks who were generally excluded from earlier training programs; ALMP training shifts toward "socialization" and low-skill-level training.

1967: The new Work Incentive Program (WIN) to put welfare recipients to work becomes the largest job-training program. Job-creation efforts in the War on Poverty are very limited; poverty and industrial parks for economic development are the main considerations, with job creation a secondary and small consideration.

1971: Emergency Employment Act leads to the job-creation boom of the 1970s which includes public-service employment, programs for youth and the elderly, and private-sector job subsidy programs. On the whole, these programs are successful: they reduce the unemployment rate by half a percentage point (Janoski: ch. 4), target the disadvantaged, and lead to increased placement and earnings for participants.

1973: Job-training programs are consolidated in CETA, but no new programs are implemented. Enrollment increases moderately until 1982. CETA programs (including Job Corps and WIN) are successful in increasing earnings and employment for participants, but training is mostly at low skill levels and for some programs takes place in stigmatized school settings.

1982: Job-creation programs are virtually eliminated; CETA is killed in Congress and replaced by the Job Training Partnership Act, a small program oriented toward employer needs as designated by bipartite (business and government) councils.

References: Janoski (1986); Wilensky (1985).

UNITED KINGDOM (8), LOW-MEDIUM SUCCESS

Summary comments. ALMP was implemented in the United Kingdom beginning in the mid-1960s and expanded in the mid-1970s, both under Labour governments; policies were cut back in 1979 and 1980 by the Thatcher government but expanded subsequently in response to high unemployment. The big problem has been dislocation between ALMP and other policies, such as fiscal and monetary policies to fight inflation and defend sterling.

Key dates and events

1948-73: Unemployment rarely exceeds 3%; employment policy consists primarily of Keynesian macroeconomic policies.

1958-62: Industrial Training Council establishes training programs to alleviate skilled manpower shortages (Moon: 23).

1964: Industrial Training Boards are set up to assess training needs and provide financial incentives.

1966: The Regional Employment Premium (REP) is established as the first plan to subsidize labor, with tax rebates (Moon: 23).

1964-70: Labour government puts large amounts of capital into sustaining jobs in industry (e.g., £20 million to Upper Clyde Shipbuilders, 1967-70).

1970-72: Manpower policies are rolled back under Heath government.

1972: REP is expanded in face of rising unemployment.

1973: Education and Training Act: industrial training grants and exemptions are strengthened; tripartite Manpower Services Commission (MSC) is created to run public employment and training and set up long-term manpower policy (Moon: 25).

1974-79: MSC activities are expanded under Labour government (Moon: 27). Job-creation efforts include the Temporary Employment Scheme (subsidies to firms to reduce layoffs) and the Job Creation Programme (work for the hardest hit in community-service jobs). Training efforts include the Training Opportunities Scheme, with 60,000 in training in 1975 (Moon: 28). Regional development policies are expanded; rescue missions to industry (e.g., British Leyland) are made with employment in mind.

1977-78: Adult job-creation subsidies are introduced (Moon: 28). Youth Opportunities Programme (YOPS) is established to combine work experience and job-creation goals, with 162,000 participants in 1978-79 (*ibid.*).

1979-83: Conservative government initially cuts back ALMP programs, but the role of MSC continues to grow in response to dramatically rising unemployment (Moon: 32). YOPS is expanded to 553,000 participants in 1981-82; adult employment subsidies are cut by 50-75%. Enterprise Allowance Programme is set up to offer subsidies for the unemployed who set up their own business.

1982-85: After the initial cuts, Thatcher government implements more extensive ALMP than the previous Labour government (Casey and Bruche: 56; McArthur and McGregor).

References: Aitken (1986); Casey and Bruche (1985); McArthur and McGregor (1986); Moon (1984).

INDUSTRIAL POLICY

JAPAN (1), HIGH SUCCESS

Summary comments. Referred to as "administrative guidance," Japanese industrial policy is highly organized and centralized through the Ministry of

International Trade and Industry (MITI) (Johnson 1982.) Developmental, managed market economy (controlled competition) is characterized by close government-business collaboration and a deliberate strategy to promote both broad and sectoral industrial development. A powerful state bureaucracy and large corporations work together for economic growth and development. MITI acts directly on the economy with budgeted funds and financial instruments. Both the state and large firms promote flexibility, specialization, and innovation in supplier networks. Labor is largely excluded from the decisionmaking process (Johnson 1982; Pempel and Tsunekawa 1979).

Key dates and events

1946-55: Adjustment of the Supply and Demand of Goods Temporary Act gives government the authority to allocate resources; Reconstruction Finance Bank supplies up to 25% of all industrial funds (Hosomi and Okumura: 125). Industrial policy is focused on reconstruction and modern industrialization; MITI is advised by tripartite Industrial Rationalization Council.

1956-73: Industrial policy concentrates first on economic independence and then on international trade (Hosomi and Okumura: 134-38). MITI orchestrates a broad developmental system using government funds, financial institutions (for loans and credit), and protective legislation to promote mergers and rationalization, encourage intense but controlled competition, keep domestic market closed while borrowing technology from abroad, promote exports, and assure an abundance of capital for critical sectors (Johnson 1982; Zysman and Tyson).

1974-85: Shift in strategy from broad developmental system to promoting growth in high-technology industries and managing an orderly decline of "losing" industries (Zysman and Tyson: 6-7). For growth industries: rationalization subsidies, tax incentives, cartels, expansion of R&D. Development of advanced technology is managed by government labs, in large directed projects involving the major corporations, with tax credits for R&D, grants, and firm collaboration (with exemption from the Anti-Monopoly Law) (Magaziner and Reich: 282-84). For declining industries: 1978 Structurally Depressed Industries Law provides loan guarantee funds to scrap capacity, recession cartels, tariff and nontariff protection (Magaziner and Reich: 275).

References: Hosomi and Okumura (1982); Johnson (1982); Magaziner and Reich (1982); Yamamura (1981); Zysman and Tyson (1984).

FRANCE (2), HIGH SUCCESS

Summary comments. "Indicative planning" was established after the war and developed into a strong, interventionist industrial policy, especially after 1958 under De Gaulle. As in Japan, the system is based on a powerful state bureaucracy, close government-business relations, and the exclusion of labor from major policymaking. Government intervention includes nationalization, regulation, and—most important—control of financial instruments for selective credit allocation. With shifts of emphasis, active industrial policy has operated continuously in the postwar period.

Key dates and events

1945-47: Governing postwar coalition establishes the Planning Commission to orchestrate active industrial policy for reconstruction and modernization, with labor support. The Treasury in the Ministry of Finance wins the dominant control of credit and thus the central position for the implementation of industrial policy (Zysman: 104-12).

1947: The Communist Party (PCF) is forced out of government; the largest labor federation (CGT) breaks with the planning process; the plan now excludes labor and evolves on a basis of close government-business collaboration.

1947-58: Industrial policy focuses on a shift from agriculture to industry, from small to large firms; government manages the evolution of industrial structure through control of credit, currency, and trade (Zysman: 146-47).

1958-68: De Gaulle comes to power, and a strengthened president in the Fifth Republic further consolidates government's planning role. Industrial policy continues; firms are forced to compete in new EEC open markets (which encourage rationalization and merger). Government in the 1960s supports the growth of large firms, "national champions," and prestige projects.

1969-80: Indicative planning remains in place, with a new accent on industrial restructuring and some "liberalization" of the economy. For growth industries, government R&D efforts are small compared to that of West Germany and Japan. The largest amount of funds goes to defense; civilian R&D focuses on prestige projects (nuclear energy, aircraft, computers) (Magaziner and Reich: 285). Government export promotion is extensive, with restructuring focused on large, complicated projects which tend to fail (e.g., computers that are unable to keep up with market developments) (pp. 278-79). Increased interagency competition regarding industrial policy leads to the 1979 establishment of CODIS, composed of several ministers under the prime minister to coordinate industrial policy (pp. 311-12). For declining industries, policies are reactive, with big subsidies to textiles, steel, shipbuilding (e.g.) and an unwillingness to abandon national champions or to lay off workers after the 1968 mass protests. In 1974 an interministerial committee (CIASI) is set up to promote restructuring, rationalization aid to individual firms for regional development, and mergers to restructure local industry (Curzon Price: 45).

1981-85: Nationalizations under the Socialist government leave the industrial policy apparatus intact, but declining sectors continue to receive huge subsidies, especially in 1981-83, with no gain in productivity. Otherwise there is an emphasis on discrete measures, loans for restructuring, financing of prototype projects, and planning agreements to target government aid to critical sectors such as electronics and machine tools. The external deficit, however, limits the total volume of credit through such targeting while unsteady, counter-productive macroeconomic policies (expansionary in 1981-82, followed by a dramatic U-turn to austerity) probably offset the positive effect of discrete measures.

References: Balassa (1985); Cohen (1977); Curzon Price (1981); Magaziner and Reich (1982); Pinder et al. (1979); Zysman (1983).

WEST GERMANY (3), HIGH SUCCESS

Summary comments. The Adenauer government (with Ludwig Erhard as Minister of Economics) embraced free-market ideology after the war, with a strong tight-money role for the Bundesbank and an emphasis on consensus in the context of liberalism. Unions accepted government policy and wage moderation in the interest of economic growth. Industrial policy has developed since 1966 (when the Socialists entered the government), with new tripartite structures including business, banks, government, and labor. Government plays an important role in promoting consensus but has no directing agency like the Japanese MITI; major decisions and implementation remain in private hands. Conflict between *Sozialpolitik* and neoliberal ideologies and groups has increased since the mid-1970s.

Key dates and events

1947-66: Period of dominant liberalism characterized by Keynesian macro-economic policies, limited formal government role, industrial decisions by banks and firms, and discussions with labor; government is in the background in a supportive but not directing role.

1966-69: Grand Coalition government establishes tripartite Concerted Action framework, which lays the consensual and information-gathering groundwork for effective industrial policy (Curzon Price: 50-51).

1969: Legislation is enacted for investment subsidies for regional industrial policy (Curzon Price: 51).

1972-82: Industrial policy is implemented by the new Ministry of Technology (for growth, advanced technology industries), the Ministry of Economics (for declining industries), and the *Länder* (strong regional development policies) (Magaziner and Reich: 312).

1972-78: Total government aid to industry (R&D, sectoral and regional, export promotion, grants, loans, tax breaks) is 26-27% of total investment and R&D (slightly higher than for France in the same period) (Magaziner and Reich: 262). For growth industries the emphasis is on R&D and major selective research funding for projects with commercial potential. From 1969 to 1979 the percentage of business R&D funded by government goes up from 14 to 20% (p. 279). Projects are screened by a joint committee of government, business, and labor, with decisions made by the Ministry of Technology emphasizing the long-term impact on the economy, especially in mechanical, electrical, and electronic engineering (p. 280). For declining industries the focus is on adjustment: regional policies, early warning, ALMP, rationalization, and advanced technology where appropriate.

References: Curzon Price (1981); Magaziner and Reich (1982); Pinder et al. (1979).

AUSTRIA (4), HIGH-MEDIUM SUCCESS

Summary comments. A consensual tripartite negotiating process has guided industrial decisionmaking since World War II; industrial policy evolves from the "social partnership" between unions and employers, with government support and participation but not necessarily leadership. The government is in a strong position to play a role in the economy: two thirds of the fifty largest corporations are nationalized, and the government position in financial markets allows investment control. Government proclaims activist industrial policy but is restrained by the need for consensus (Katzenstein 1984: 143, 157). Government has used industrial policy effectively, but not in the dirigiste sense as in France and Japan. Broad "Austro-Keynesian" policies have predominated, as opposed to specific and sectoral industrial policy. The policy mix has been aptly described as a small-step "reactive and flexible policy of industrial adjustment" (Katzenstein 1985: 27).

Key dates and events

1947-60: Government policy (credit allocation, direct and indirect investment subsidies) is used as effective support for reconstruction and modernization in the context of tripartite negotiations.

1961-68: Gradual industrial restructuring is organized by business-labor agreement; government instruments are used to support and implement tripartite decisions, with government following the business-labor lead (Katzenstein 1984: 157).

1968-74: Strong export-led growth minimizes the need for industrial policy, although government continues to make attempts at industrial policy. In 1969 legislation encourages mergers for economic efficiency and competitiveness (Katzenstein 1985: 74).

1970-80: Small-step adjustment prevails, with an emphasis on a macroeconomic approach (e.g., hard currency) as opposed to direct, sectoral industrial policy, and job protection and social security as opposed to cuts in wages and working conditions. But investment subsidies rise substantially in response to a growing need for adjustment, increasing from U.S.$96 million in 1970 to $548 million in 1980 (Katzenstein 1984: 56). Increasingly government influences the allocation of capital to affect the structure of industry, to readjust while cushioning the labor-market shock; the emphasis is on investment growth (Katzenstein 1985: 75-76).

Late 1970s-1985: The labor-business social partnership persists, marked by negotiated decisionmaking in which government participates but does not command. Gradual industrial adjustment proceeds in a context of job protection. Keynesian strategy is being reoriented toward structural readjustment based on a fair sharing of transition costs, skill upgrading (especially computer-related skills), and regional technology centers for small and medium-sized firms. Experimental regional consortia include the heads of factory councils, chambers of labor and industry, local mayors, and parliamentary representatives (Sabel).

References: Katzenstein (1984, 1985); Sabel (1984).

SWEDEN (5), MEDIUM SUCCESS

Summary comments. Sweden has not developed active industrial policy in the usual sense. The Rehn/Meidner model, implemented around 1960, aimed to promote competitiveness and economic adjustment through a combination of wage solidarity and tight fiscal policy, squeeze out noncompetitive firms, and increase the profitability of competitive firms. Centralized collective bargaining (de facto incomes policy) and ALMP to promote geographical and occupational mobility have been central to this strategy. But this adds up to an industrial policy of sorts (Martin 1979: 105), as the set of policies aims explicitly to force competitiveness and continually restructure Swedish industry. After 1970 more typical interventionist industrial policy aimed to save declining industries and make them competitive again; since 1982 policy efforts have been more proactive and apparently successful. Industrial policy in Sweden, to the extent that it exists, has been tightly linked to labor-market and wage policies, and all have been developed through tripartite negotiation.

Key dates and events

1944: The LO and Social Democratic Party (SAP) develop an active industrial policy plan, but this is defeated by employers and never implemented, as SAP loses seats in 1948 and is forced to govern in coalition with the Agrarian Party from 1951 to 1957.

1951: The LO develops the Rehn/Meidner model as an alternative to central economic planning (the French model).

1957-60: Rehn/Meidner model adopted and implemented.

1965: Regional investment subsidies increase substantially in response to protest regarding the decline of jobs and industry in the north and central areas as a result of the implementation of the Rehn/Meidner model. These subsidies (which serve both job-creation and industrial policy goals) continue to rise through the 1970s (Rehn: 78-79).

1966-67: "New industrial policy" is proclaimed with state investment bank, R&D agencies, and regional and sectoral planning apparatus—but it does not amount to much (Martin 1979: 110).

1969: AB Statsforetag is established as a state financial holding company to save weak firms. This marks a symbolic end to the unconditional commitment to adjustment and labor-market mobility (Haber: 242) and the beginning of increasing government intervention to save jobs, firms, and industries.

1970-82: Government intervention increases in the face of difficult economic problems and adjustment requirements, but industrial policy is still reactive and ad hoc, focused on saving jobs and investments in major industries such as steel and ships and in threatened regions (Belfrage and Molleryd: 177; Scharpf 1981: 30). In the late 1970s, the government decides on large capital grants to selected companies. The grants are described as both industrial policy (for structural change and adaptation) and ALMP (job protection and creation) (Henning: 202). But for these years employment goals seem to take precedence over industrial policy goals (Henning: 197, 205).

1982-86: With the election of a new Social Democratic government, Sweden shifts to a more affirmative, adjustment-oriented industrial policy. The government cuts subsidies to declining industries and successfully encourages the rapid introduction of advanced technology in industry. As a result, both exports and growth are up by the mid-1980s and the Swedish economy appears to be improving.

References: Belfrage and Molleryd (1984); Haber (1982); Henning (1984); Martin (1979); Rehn (1985); Scharpf (1981).

NETHERLANDS (6), MEDIUM-LOW SUCCESS

Summary comments. Except for postwar reconstruction, the Netherlands has not had organized industrial policy, although the development of such policy is now on the agenda. Exceptions include regional policy, support for weak industries, and some reactive industrial policy. Dramatic economic growth in the 1950s and 1960s along with an abundance of natural gas in the 1970s have deferred the discussion of active industrial policy. For most of the postwar period, policy focus has been on growth, employment, and redistribution rather than industrial structure. For the past decade, moves toward industrial policy have been complicated by political conflict and the weakening of the corporatist decisionmaking apparatus.

Key dates and events

1945-50: Effective government industrial policy, based on tripartite agreement, promotes reconstruction and contributes to the 1950s takeoff of economic growth. The Central Plan Bureau is established in 1945 but never gets off the ground as a planning agency (this was a Socialist plan opposed by others); instead it becomes an effective forecast agency (Wolinetz 1983: 8).

Early 1950s: Tripartite industrial boards are established under the Social and Economic Council (SER) but only in weak industries (Wolinetz 1983: 9). Active industrial policy is replaced by active promotional policy: financial and technical assistance is provided to industry to encourage investment and create jobs—any jobs (p. 9).

Mid-1950s-1970: Active government industrial intervention gives way to passive or reactive policies of the Ministry of Economic Affairs during the "economic miracle" years. Corporatist structure (including the tripartite SER and bipartite Foundation of Labor [FL]) focuses on wage restraints backed by social welfare. Government policy is directed at jobs, price stability, balance of payments, growth, and redistribution—*not* the structure of industry. Ad hoc subsidies for declining industries expand in the 1960s, with improvisation the rule (Katzenstein 1985: 65).

1971-80: The Netherlands Restructuring Corporation (NEHEM) is established in 1971 to oversee restructuring in weak sectors and to work with firms and unions, but it is not given enough authority and is ineffective in the face of growing firm/union conflicts. In spite of some success in making industries competitive (Curzon Price: 71) and the promotion of some high-tech sectors (Katzenstein 1985: 66), on the whole NEHEM does not achieve restructuring goals (Wolinetz 1983).

1980-85: Discussion of focused, active industrial policy finally begins, later than in most countries due to (1) natural gas, which muted the 1970s energy crisis, and (2) increasingly conflictual domestic political configurations. But government has few levers over finance and industrial capital (Wolinetz 1985: 49). Dutch elites today see industrial policy as led by an expert commission, not by SER or FL, in which partners have become opponents.

References: Curzon Price (1981); Katzenstein (1985); Wolinetz (1983, 1985).

UNITED KINGDOM (7), LOW SUCCESS

Summary comments. Beginning in the early 1960s, the United Kingdom has tried all sorts of industrial policies, depending on the political swings between Labour and Conservative governments and economic fluctuations. In spite of many attempts, these policies have had very little success.

Key dates and events

1945-60: The early postwar years are characterized by dismantling of the wartime economy, nationalization under a Labour government (1945-51), and expansion of the welfare state, but no active industrial policy, especially after 1951, when the Conservatives return to power under a free-enterprise banner. The United Kingdom is one of only a few industrialized societies without an active industrial policy for reconstruction; a broad postwar national consensus developed for the welfare state and Keynesian fiscal and monetary policies for the regulation of aggregate demand, without industrial policy-type government intervention.

1961-70: The National Economic Development Corporation (NEDC, or Neddy) is established in 1961, a tripartite agency for economic information-gathering and planning which later spawns thirty-nine "little Neddies" for specific sectors (Curzon Price: 57). These years are characterized by attempts at French-style planning (but on a tripartite basis) in response to slow growth, balance of payments deficits, and adjustment problems. Neddy's role is expanded by the Labour government, but efforts are undermined by conflict within the government and a serious disjuncture with government macro-economic policies (based on defense of the sterling) (Blank: 117-19). A short-lived National Plan in the mid-1960s is followed by the 1967-70 tripartite Industrial Reorganization Corporation to promote mergers and rationaliza-tion (Pinder et al.: 34). £150 million per year is spent by this agency for advanced technology industry, but conflict leads to its dissolution (Magaziner and Reich: 300-302).

1970-72: Conservative government favors the free market and opposes planning, but mounting economic problems and conflicts lead to the famous 1972 Heath U-turn.

1972-79: Industrial policy efforts increase under both Conservative and Labour governments. In 1972 the Industry Act directs public capital to private firms as investment to improve competitiveness and productivity. But from 1972 on, the pattern of British industrial policy is to inject large subsidies into troubled firms (British Leyland gets the biggest chunk) (Pinder et al.: 34). Employment and industry are propped up without achieving stated goals of growth or adjustment. In 1975 the National Enterprise Board (NEB) is set up as a new central agency to continue 1972 policies by supplying state equity financing to promising and declining industries (Curzon Price: 59). From 1972 to 1980 government R&D expenditures drop from $300 million to $160 million, as R&D is privatized (Magaziner and Reich: 284). In the 1970s strong regional policies are enacted but are not selective; many non-viable projects are funded.

1979-85: NEB merges with old NEDC (1979); policy now aims at high-risk, high-tech capital grants for new projects, such as the Microelectronic Industrial Sup-port Scheme. Begun in 1978, it receives £120 million in 1980 and 1981 to en-courage firms to use microprocessors in products and processes (Magaziner and Reich: 303). Thatcher government policies aim to phase out subsidies to private firms. The key strategy is to break labor's power and impose or unleash a long-term company-led industrial readjustment. Prospects remain uncertain.

References: Blank (1978); Curzon Price (1981); Magaziner and Reich (1982); Pinder et al. (1979).

UNITED STATES (8), LOW SUCCESS

Summary comments. To the extent that the U.S. government has had policies toward industry, they have been *macroeconomic* fiscal and monetary policies (broad demand- and/or supply-side policies); focused on *national security* (defense spending) and *space* programs; and *reactive* for troubled industries (quotas, Orderly Marketing Agreements, trigger prices for specific sectors, occasional bailouts, as for Chrysler and Lockheed). The main exception has been in agricultural policy. In addition, the states have enacted a potpourri of often competing policies to encourage local industry.

To the extent that the U.S. government has promoted R&D, it has done so mostly through the Department of Defense, NASA, and for agriculture.

With these exceptions, the United States has had no active industrial policy — i.e., coordinated attempts to manage structural economic/industrial change. The trend under Reagan (with deregulation, ATT divestiture, declining union strength, budget cutbacks for many social programs and increases for defense, etc.) is to let the market decide, even more so than in the past, and to use a loose fiscal policy in the hope of indirectly increasing investment and growth.

INCOMES POLICY

AUSTRIA (1), HIGH SUCCESS

Summary comments. Austria has had continuous incomes policies since 1947. Success has been based on social partnership in the form of voluntary agreements between centralized labor and employer federations, with government presence and facilitation. Close ties of labor to a strong Socialist party has given labor an active voice in social and other policies, which is important for labor's incomes policy cooperation. The Austrian Trade Union Federation (ÖGB) has taken a broad view of economic growth: wages have been tied to productivity and the requirements of the economy; redistribution has been seen as a legislative, not a wage-bargaining problem (Flanagan et al.: 54-81). Rank-and-file revolt has been minimized through a combination of the centralization of authority in the ÖGB with decentralized local negotiations and the integration of shop stewards into Socialist party and labor organizations (p. 80). But Austrian corporatism is more rigid and less participatory than the Norwegian or Swedish systems, with fewer local adaptations.

Key dates and events

1947-55: Main interest organizations (ÖGB and Chambers of Labor, Commerce, and Agriculture) negotiate agreements on both wages and prices, seeking growth without inflation.

1956: The Parity Commission is established, the basic incomes policy institution in which labor and business meet on a voluntary basis for consensual decision-making. Government is present but does not vote. The Commission's wage subcommittee considers collective bargaining after union proposals are screened by the ÖGB (Flanagan et al.: 58-60; Driscoll 1982a: 14-15).

1956-85: This system has functioned uninterrupted, with wage negotiations at yearly or eighteen-month intervals. Government response to mid-1970s inflation is the "hard-currency option" (schilling tied to the German mark), at the suggestion of the ÖGB. This keeps wages down to the level of productivity increase (Flanagan et al.: 45-47). Incomes policy is closely tied to discussions and implementation of other policies such as social, tax, and employment (Katzenstein 1985: 92).

References: Driscoll (1982a); Flanagan, Soskice, and Ulman (1983); Katzenstein (1984, 1985).

WEST GERMANY (2), HIGH SUCCESS

Summary comments. West Germany has had continuous incomes policies, informal or formal, since the early 1950s. Unions have accepted restrained collective bargaining gains in a context of centralized labor and business federations which share economywide perspectives and goals: price stability, full employment, growth. Social partnership has included labor in a secondary, not equal, role. Unions claim that restraint has paid off in economic progress for members. Government has always communicated its views to collective bargaining participants regarding acceptable wage levels.

Key dates and events

1950-65: Modest role for informal incomes policy within the dominant free-market ideology and policies; effective exhortations from the Chancellor's office and Bundesbank regarding wages; employers in a dominant position under conservative governments (Flanagan et al.: 275-79).

1966-69: "Concerted Action" formal incomes policy is promoted by the Grand Coalition government, which includes Socialists. The tradeoff for unions is a commitment to full employment and institutional equality (tripartite meetings for consensus on wages) (*ibid.*, p. 280).

1969-73: Rising worker dissatisfaction with the tradeoff leads to rank-and-file rebellion and wage increases. Concerted Action meetings continue through this period (until 1977) and may have helped hold down wage increases in the face of worker militancy (*ibid.*, p. 286).

1977-85: Unions pull out of Concerted Action meetings after a new Codetermination Law fails to pass and from dissatisfaction with the tradeoffs for wage restraint (*ibid.*, pp. 284-85). Incomes policy continues on an informal basis; union restraint continues in face of inflation and rising unemployment (pp. 287-88). In 1984 the largest postwar strike leads to modest gains in spite of high unemployment and foreshadows a possible weakening of the social partnership.

References: Flanagan, Soskice, and Ulman (1983); A. Wilson (1982).

SWEDEN (3), HIGH SUCCESS

Summary comments. Sweden has had effective de facto incomes policies throughout the postwar period. Highly centralized collective bargaining has substituted for formal incomes policy, making effective wage restraint possible in a high-employment economy (Flanagan et al.: 305; Katzenstein 1985: 50). Negotiations are bilateral between labor and employers, but government plays a strong behind-the-scenes role, offering tradeoffs for wage restraint. LO (labor) and SAF (employers) are both centralized; labor has political strength, an economywide perspective, and a "solidaristic" (egalitarian) wage policy; close relation is seen by all parties between wage levels and labor-market, industrial, and social policies (Addison: 238-39).

Key dates and events

1946-52: Tripartite wage restraint cooperation ends in worker discontent, wage drift, and big raises triggered by the Korean War. LO and SAF agree to central collective bargaining as an emergency measure (Flanagan et al: 305).

1956: Central, economywide collective bargaining is regularized between LO and SAF, with government in support role providing economic forecasts (*ibid.*, p. 305).

1956-70: Continuous de facto incomes policies based on centralized collective bargaining; government remains behind the scenes, providing forecasts and arranging ALMP and social transfers as tradeoffs for wage restraint.

1970-81: Increasing government involvement in the bargaining process, especially in 1970, 1973, and 1975-80 (*ibid.*, pp. 349-50). Government announces social transfers and tax changes (beginning in 1973) *prior* to the start of collective bargaining (p. 350). This period is characterized by mounting problems of competitiveness and economic adjustment and growing worker dissatisfaction, especially among the higher paid, in the face of solidaristic wage policies and labor-market mobility policies. LO responds by pushing for industrial democracy, job security, and co-ownership (investment funds) as new tradeoffs for wage restraint (pp. 332-36; Martin 1984: 248ff.).

1982-85: Movement occurs toward decentralized collective bargaining and a breakdown of incomes policy. The salaried unions in the private sector (PTK) break away in 1982, metal workers in 1983. But PTK and LO agree to coordinate again with SAF in 1984, and government continues as an active partner arranging tradeoffs (e.g., 1985 agreement to cut inflation to 3% while wages rise 5%). In 1984 the government establishes investment funds as a move toward labor co-ownership, in part as a tradeoff for wage restraint; strong management resistance persists. (Wilensky interviews.)

References: Addison (1981); Flanagan, Soskice, and Ulman (1983); Katzenstein (1985); Martin (1984).

JAPAN (4), HIGH-MEDIUM SUCCESS

Summary comments. Japan has combatted inflation mainly through fiscal and monetary policy, backed up by price controls. Government has intervened in only a limited way in wage negotiations; wage moderation has occurred in a context of social partnership and enterprise unionism. Company-dominated industrial relations have been harmonious in the absence of strong trade unions. Wage raises are generally held to the level of productivity increase; cost-push inflation has been avoided. Government has been behind the scenes, quietly supporting wage restraint. Government occasionally jawbones, meeting with labor leaders prior to spring negotiations to communicate inflation goals; with no force of law, this has proven an effective form of pressure. "In short, Japan has no formal wage policy. It does, however, have a social contract buttressed by the structure of its industrial relations that invokes a kind of soft incomes policy" (Nanto: 42; compare Levine).

Key dates and events

1950-73: The system of industry/government partnership and enterprise unionism has moderate success in restraining wages, although there are periods when the government seeks to raise income (and thus purchasing power). Inflation is higher for most of this period than in the United States.

1974: Labor gets a 32% wage increase; government seriously considers formal incomes policy but decides to rely on enterprise unionism (Nanto: 40).

1975-85: The system experiences much success as both inflation and wage raises are held down. We can infer increased government pressure because of the 1974 wage explosion (Nanto: 42); new tripartite joint consultation machinery is established (JIL 1979b: 29-30); tripartite and bipartite meetings regarding wages and the needs of the economy become more regular and frequent (Taira and Levine: 249-52).

References: JIL (1979b); Levine (1983); Nanto (1982); Taira and Levine (1985).

NETHERLANDS (5), MEDIUM SUCCESS

Summary comments. The Netherlands has had active incomes policies throughout the postwar period. The wage bargaining structure assures government participation through the Board of Government Mediators. In spite of divided trade unions and political fragmentation, a tripartite postwar social partnership has underpinned government efforts at wage restraint. A tendency toward government-imposed wage restraint in the past decade developed from the tripartite framework and has been tacitly accepted by both organized labor and business.

Key dates and events

1945: Extraordinary Decree on Labor Relations prohibits employers from paying more than wage levels approved by the Board of Government Mediators (Flanagan et al: 103). The bipartite Foundation of Labor is established and works with the board to set wage guidelines and approve collective bargaining agreements (Wolinetz 1985: 15).

1945-54: The tripartite framework for agreements holds wages down to the level of consumer price rises (Flanagan et al.: 107). Formal incomes policy is seen as indispensable for industrial growth in an open, vulnerable economy (Katzenstein 1985: 49).

1954-59: Increasing union pressure leads to a relaxation of wage policies (including more pay differentials), with continued restraint (Flanagan et al.: 108).

1959-62: Continued success, now marred by increasing opposition; confessional unions and employers favor decentralized bargaining and continue to demand wider pay differentials (*ibid.*, p. 112).

1963-65: Wages increase substantially as consensus begins to break down (*ibid.*, p. 116). For the rest of the decade, wages rise more than productivity and inflation heats up.

1967-70: Mandatory government wage policy put in effect (*ibid.*, p. 119). Industry moves toward free collective bargaining, but government retains the power to reject and extend contracts and freeze wages. From this time on, government plays an important role in setting wages as business and labor are no longer able to reach central wage accords (Wolinetz 1985).

1970-81: Industrial conflict increases from 1971 to 1973; there are major strikes in the building trades and factory occupations to prevent closures. Strike rates decline from 1973 to 1977. Government wage freezes alternate with a new generation of social partnership incomes policies, with tradeoffs on social policies, hours, taxes, and subsidies for employers. A pattern emerges: collective bargaining failures are followed by government-established norms, which are then tacitly accepted by all (Flanagan et al.: 153).

1981-85: Government pursues uncompensated incomes policy: wage restraint is combined with deflation and social transfer cutbacks. Incomes policy continues as a function of government, with tacit consent from both employers and unions (Wolinetz 1983: 24).

References: Driscoll (1982b); Flanagan, Soskice, and Ulman (1983); Katzenstein (1985); Wolinetz (1983, 1985).

FRANCE (6), MEDIUM SUCCESS

Summary comments. France has had no negotiated incomes policy in the postwar period and no direct government intervention to hold down wages except in two periods: 1964-68 and 1976-78. Long-term wage restraint has been due to employer strength and labor weakness. In a context of close government-employer relations and a divided labor movement, employers set wages. There was virtually no effective collective bargaining prior to 1968 (Flanagan et al.: 573). The postwar pattern has been that wage increases are granted when necessary to reduce unrest, and inflation is then allowed to reduce gains. Both the CGT (the strongest labor federation) and the CNPF (the employers' federation) have opposed incomes policy.

Key dates and events

1945-47: Under the *tripartisme* government, French planning is inaugurated with CGT support. This is a period of labor cooperation on wages and other matters to restore productivity to the economy (Flanagan et al.: 575-76).

1947: CGT cooperation with the government ends as the Communist Party (PCF) is forced out of the governing coalition. Exclusion of labor from government policymaking is solidified in the 1950s; employers dominate the wage-setting process.

1963-64: Wage raises in response to strike waves and a tight labor market lead the De Gaulle government to attempt incomes policy, with no success; the CGT is not interested and what occurs has been termed a "dialogue of mutes" (Flanagan et al.: 599; Addision: 224).

1964-68: Government-imposed wage restraint becomes central to De Gaulle's policy to build up French industry (Flanagan et al.: 600-605).

1969-76: Workers get wage raises and expanded collective bargaining after the rebellion of 1968, with still no negotiated or even tacit incomes policy. The government goal is to move toward collective bargaining and incomes policy and detach unions from their political parties. This fails; both the CGT and CFDT (the smaller labor federation linked to the Socialists) oppose incomes policy as the Left approaches power (*ibid.*, pp. 606-7, 628-29).

1976-78: The Giscard/Barre government imposes wage restraint, by government fiat in the public sector and government pressure in the private sector (*ibid.*, p. 625; Addison: 226).

1978-81: Policies of economic "liberalization" characterize this period, but collective bargaining remains limited; a loosened wage restraint policy has only limited success and no union agreement (Flanagan et al.: 639-45).

1981-82: The new Socialist government raises the minimum wage and encourages wage raises (Sellier: 184).

1982-85: About-face austerity policies are inaugurated, with a six-month wage and price freeze; government pressures industry and labor to hold down wages, with tradeoffs for labor (such as institutional security and quality of worklife) (Sellier: 191-93, 208).

References: Addison (1981); Flanagan, Soskice, and Ulman (1983); Sellier (1985).

UNITED KINGDOM (7), MEDIUM-LOW SUCCESS

Summary comments. The United Kingdom has experimented with incomes policy in several periods since World War II, but with limited and always short-term success. Best results have come with Labour in power backed by the Trades Union Congress (TUC). Policies have been undermined by persistent economic stagnation and inflation, low growth, sterling crises, the alternation of governments, decentralization in the TUC, and a decentralized industrial relations system with plenty of room for uneven wage drift.

Key dates and events

1948-50: Nonstatutory incomes policy promoted by the Labour government, supported by the TUC; TUC support withdrawn in 1950 due to wage drift and rank-and-file dissatisfaction (Flanagan et al.: 377).

1951-64: Although there is no incomes policy during these years, tacit wage restraint is accepted by the TUC with a Conservative government in power. The public-sector "pay pause" in 1961-62 is the first explicit attempt at incomes policy (*ibid.*, p. 386).

1964-70: Continuous, explicit incomes policy, in one form or other, is administered by the tripartite National Board for Prices and Incomes (NBPI), a major government effort. TUC and Labour government cooperation during this period ends with internal conflicts; the effects of wage restraint vary from sector to sector (*ibid.*, pp. 388-97; Ingham: 267-70).

1970-72: The new Heath government is at first hostile to incomes policy, attempting wage restraint through guidelines (Ingham: 271).

1972-73: Heath U-turn includes an attempt at incomes policy, with some passive union cooperation; this policy effort is wrecked by the miners' strike (Flanagan et al.: 408-18).

1974-79: Continuous explicit incomes policies are negotiated between the TUC and Labour government (*ibid.*, pp. 418-36; Ingham: 278-79). But the proclaimed "social contract" eludes Prime Minister Wilson; Prime Minister Callaghan officially pronounces it dead.

1979-85: The Thatcher government opposes incomes policy; wages are held down by deflationary fiscal and monetary policies and direct challenges to trade union power (Flanagan et al: 436-37).

References: Blank (1978); Flanagan, Soskice, and Ulman (1983); Ingham (1981).

UNITED STATES (8), LOW SUCCESS

Summary comments. The U.S. government has made four attempts at organized incomes policy since World War II, with only limited and short-term success. One major problem for incomes policy is that wage decisions are highly dispersed throughout the economy. As of 1979, only 30% of private-sector workers were covered by collective bargaining agreements, which are often local-level agreements (Pencavel: 156-57). The AFL-CIO has no authority to enforce incomes policy agreements.

Key dates and events

1950-53: The tripartite Wage Stabilization Board (WSB) is established during the Korean War. Wage restraint efforts begin with jawboning and a freeze on auto prices and autoworkers' pay. In 1951 there is a general wage and price freeze for one month, with limited increases subsequently allowed. Controls are relaxed in 1952. WSB authority is undermined when coal employers and the UMW negotiate higher-than-allowed raises. Formal decontrol comes in 1953 (Pencavel: 160).

1962-66: So-called "guideposts" are established under Kennedy to restrain inflation in a time of expansive fiscal and monetary policies. With no force of law, they rely on an educational effect to keep wage raises at the level of productivity increase; compliance is monitored by the Council of Economic Advisors, with only a small staff. In 1966 airline machinists and employers negotiate raises which defy government policy and lead to termination of the guideposts (Pencavel: 161).

1971-74: Wage and price controls are established under Nixon. Phase I is a ninety-day freeze. Phase II is marked by establishment of the Pay Board, which is tripartite until 1972, when labor withdraws due to dissatisfaction with the Price Commission. Allowed wage increases are based on productivity increase plus cost of living. In Phase III, controls are relaxed in 1973 under the Cost-of-Living Council (a merger of the Pay Board and Price Commission). Sharp inflation leads to a new sixty-day freeze; subsequent big increases in food and energy prices prove beyond government control. In Phase IV, controls are phased out (Pencavel: 162-63).

1978-80: Pay and price standards are promulgated as one Carter government response to inflation; maximum permissible wage increases are set (originally 7% for wages), then modified piecemeal to accommodate major collective bargaining agreements. But there are no penalties for noncompliance and inflation continues. In 1979 labor is invited to participate, and a tripartite pay advisory committee is established. A new standard is set (8.5%), but no impact on inflation is demonstrated (Pencavel: 164-65).

References: Dunlop (1977); Katzenstein (1985); Pencavel (1981); Rees (1979).

Appendix B

MEASURES OF ECONOMIC PERFORMANCE
AND ENERGY DEPENDENCE

The measures reported in all the tables and in the text are from Wilensky (in preparation), which contains a detailed discussion of nineteen rich democracies with a population of one million or more in 1966. Social-security effort in Table 1 is based on data in ILO (1972, 1976, 1979, 1981). The two columns of figures are a twenty-five-year (1950-74) average of annual social-security spending as a percent of GNP at factor cost and a comparable three-year (1977-79) average, with minor adjustments. These data are a good clue to social spending other than education; their uses and limits are discussed in Wilensky (1975: 2-9, 125-28).

Economic performance measures are as follows:

Economic growth. Average annual real growth of GDP per capita, 1950-74. Except for Japan, the averages are for the twenty-four years 1951-74; for Japan the averages cover 1954-74. The source for this period and for later periods is the UN Statistical Office (various years).

Inflation. Average year-to-year percentage increase in the GNP price deflator for the twenty-four years 1951-74 and the five years 1975-79. Source: UN Statistical Office, *Yearbook of National Accounts Statistics, 1979*, vol. 2, table 10a. For 1980-84: OECD (1986). We averaged year-to-year changes.

Unemployment. For 1950-74, we computed three-year averages of the unemployment rate centered on 1950, 1955, 1960, 1965, 1970, and 1973. The average of these six figures is reported in these tables. (A later check on averages for all years showed almost identical figures.) Post-shock figures are averages of the relevant five years. Sources: For 1950-70, OECD (1963, 1975). For 1950 and 1955 three-year averages for Sweden, France, and Austria, OECD data were supplemented by UN/ILO (various years). For 1975-79 the source is OECD (1985a); for 1980-84, OECD (1985b). For 1975-79, figures for Japan and Sweden are based on total labor force, other countries on civilian labor force only. We are grateful to René Bertrand, head of OECD's Economic Statistics and National Accounts Division, for supplying unpublished adjustments in these data to compensate for differing methods of measuring unemployment: "Unemployment Rates Adjusted to International Concepts, 1950-74, Nine Countries" (mimeo). In a comparison of different sources, the only discrepancy big enough to substantially affect the rank order of unemployment for nineteen countries was for Denmark. Its average unemployment rate 1950-74 (1.4%) ranks fourteenth based on OECD (1975), while the average based on the unpublished OECD source (3.1%) ranks it fourth. It turned out that the unpublished adjustments were accurate (consistent with national labor surveys as well), while the published ones were erroneously low; we used the higher figure. For Israel, all years, the source is UN/ILO (various years).

The summary index of economic performance in Table 1. This index weighs the three measures roughly equally. For nineteen countries in the larger study, of which this is a part, average annual real growth of GDP per capita, inflation, and unemployment are each given a score of 0 (low), 1 (medium), and 2 (high) based on averages for each of three periods.

Rather than dividing the nineteen countries arbitrarily by, say, quintiles (so that a one tenth of one percent difference might separate high from medium), we used natural break points. We then added the three scores for a summary performance score ranging from 0 to 6 (poor to excellent). Thus for 1950-74 West Germany gets 1 for unemployment (medium), 2 for growth (high), and 2 for inflation (low) for a summary score of 5 (for this period and comparing all nineteen countries, excellent). The United States gets 0 for unemployment (high), 0 for growth (low), and 2 for inflation (low) for a summary score of 2 (fair-to-poor). The same procedure is used for subsequent periods. This summary index avoids the assumption that high inflation is worse than high unemployment or high real growth is more important than avoiding high unemployment and/or inflation (a problem with commonly used "misery indexes").

Is increased employment as important as decreased unemployment? Should we not add job creation rates to unemployment as a measure of economic performance linked to public policies? In the ideological confrontation of the late 1970s and 1980s "neoconservatives" and many mainstream economists have asserted that the United States, despite its high rates of unemployment, has performed much better than the measures of unemployment, growth, and inflation suggest because it has created jobs at a faster rate. Their arguments, stated in their most forceful form, boil down to two: (1) the labor-force pressure argument, and (2) the total opportunity argument. Whatever the causes, they assert, countries like the United States that presumably have the fastest growing labor force and the fastest growing labor-force participation rates are under greater pressure to create jobs. If, like the United States, they run 7-10 percent unemployment rates but create jobs fast for new entrants (illegal and legal immigrants, women, and a large, maturing baby-boom cohort), they should be rated high or medium on labor-market performance, not low. Regarding total opportunity, even if the jobs created in the United States are low-paid service jobs, even if they are created as a product of lower real wages, they are real opportunities for those who take them—young people, minorities, women, immigrants. They make otherwise unmanageable social problems manageable. It is better to keep teenagers working at McDonald's than pushing dope on the street.

The laissez-faire "job creationists" seldom confront the issues posed by close students of labor markets. The counterargument boils down to a judgment of (1) what kind of comparisons are appropriate, and (2) what kind of a political economy is desirable. Although a thorough analysis of these issues is beyond the scope of this monograph and the relevant data are limited, we can sketch the counterarguments and indicate the complexity of the issues.

Before judging the merits of different rates of job creation, we must control for the *need* for jobs as indicated by dependency ratios, women's work as it relates to family breakup rates, and the timing of previous increases in female labor-force participation. If a country has a large and increasing percentage of persons of retirement age (e.g., West Germany) and/or many very young people not seeking jobs, it will not typically evidence a big growth in employment and an increasing labor-force participation rate and should not be expected to. If a country has a relatively high rate of family breakup (in 1980 the United States had the *highest* divorce rate among nineteen rich democracies) and it lacks a family policy to prevent the feminization of poverty (the United States stands alone on this, with women heading broken homes comprising almost half the poor households in the early 1980s), then it will accelerate the rate of female labor-force participation. While much of the increase in working women is a product of changing sex roles, lower fertility, and is uncoerced, some of the increase is forced by family breakup, a major cause of pre-transfer poverty. We cannot sort out the coercive versus voluntary percentage of female labor-force participation quantitatively and cross-nationally, but it obviously applies to the 1975-86 record of the United States. Further, much of labor-market performance in the 1980s is a product of earlier performance. Thus the *low* female labor-force participation rates in the United States of the 1950s and early 1960s were matched by *high* female participation rates among several smaller European democracies (Sweden, Switzerland, Finland) and Japan. Therefore, the greater increase in female labor-force participation of the United States in the 1970s and 1980s in part reflects a U.S. catchup with general tendencies toward lower fertility and higher participation. Conversely, if a country starts high in women working, it has a slower rate of increase. In short, in any comparison of increased employment as a measure of economic success, we must take account of high versus low starting points.

Regarding migrant workers as a percentage of the civilian labor force and hence as a pressure for job creation, two points must be considered. First, shortages of labor inspired most of this migration in both Europe and North America. It is not as though the rich countries were reluctant victims of external pressure. Second, after the slowdown of 1975-84, if the heavy users of guest workers were successful in sending them home, then the United States deserves some handicapping credit; its large open borders expose it to unique job-creation pressures. But, in fact, most of the guest workers in Europe, despite pressures to leave, stayed. Further, the United States is not uniquely exposed. Estimates of migrant workers as a percentage of the civilian labor force in the year closest to 1973 suggest that the United States ranked sixth among sixteen rich democracies, with about 7 percent, behind Switzerland (29 percent), West Germany (9.4 percent), France (9.0 percent), Austria (7.8 percent), and the United Kingdom (7.3 percent). By the early 1980s, the United States appears to have maintained its rank as slightly above the median (among eighteen cases for which we found data on net migration 1980-83).

Most important is the question 'What kind of political economy is desirable?" There is consensus about the desirability of real growth, low inflation, and low unemployment. There is little consensus about the meaning of growth of labor-force participation or jobs added. If employment is expanded by the rapid creation of low-paid service jobs, an increasing number of them part-time jobs taken by people looking for full-time work; a steady drop in real wages; and increases in rates of family breakup (forcing single parents to work more than they wish to), while productivity increases fade and international competitiveness and trade balances deteriorate, we can ask, "Is this progress?" The better strategy is to upgrade the labor force and improve the technical and social organization of work and thereby increase productivity and product quality, generally moving upscale in exports, rather than aping the labor-intensive newly industrializing countries (NICs) such as Korea and Hong Kong. Further, if real-wage decreases are to be achieved by sustaining high unemployment rates and/or by union busting (United States under Reagan, United Kingdom under Thatcher), we incur all the costs of mass insecurity, industrial conflict, ungovernability, and unproductive welfare spending evident in the larger study of which this is a part (Wilensky 1976, 1983, 1985). If to this perverse combination we add a high level of family breakup and the feminization of poverty, should we label the brew "a superior record of job creation?"

Finally, no one has either firmly established or disconfirmed a *long*-term American trend toward low-wage jobs in or out of the service sector. Suppose we adopt the view that all si₃ns of this earnings deterioration since 1973 are not a trend but a cyclical pattern reflecting the sharp increase in the percentage of low-wage workers in the recession years of 1975 and 1981-82. In cross-national perspective recessions *are* the issue. And the depth and duration of recessions as they shape long-run productivity, growth, and standards of living are best captured by the real growth and unemployment data reported in the text.

In short, to assert that the United States, despite its high unemployment rate, is an outstanding job creator from 1975 to 1985 is to ignore national differences in demographic structure, the history of female labor-force participation, family breakup, and migration, as well as variation in systems of retirement and education and training. Buried in that assertion is a set of values regarding desirable strategies for political and economic development about which there is no agreement.

Vulnerability to oil shocks as a handicap. Two measures are "liquid fuels as a percentage of total energy consumption," 1970 and 1978, and "energy production as a percentage of energy consumption," 1970 and 1978 (United

Nations 1974, 1979). "Liquid fuels" is mainly oil but also includes natural gas liquids (e.g., liquid hydrocarbon mixtures recovered through the processing of wet natural gas). "Energy production" includes solid fuels such as coal and lignite, liquid fuels such as oil and natural gas liquids, natural gas, and hydro-nuclear power. Combining the two measures in an index, equally weighting the two measures for 1978, and scoring each high (2), medium (1), and low (0), we see the following rank for most to least vulnerable to oil shocks (based on nineteen countries):

Japan	4	High vulnerability
Sweden	3	Medium-high
Austria	2	Medium
West Germany	2	Medium
France	2	Medium
United Kingdom	0	Low
Netherlands	0	Low
United States	0	Low

Of the eight countries in this monograph only the Netherlands and the United Kingdom lessened their energy dependence substantially from 1973 to 1978. Among the nineteen rich democracies, both moved from medium to low vulnerability.

Thus in view of their great vulnerability to oil shocks, we can give special credit to Japan and Sweden. In the face of tough odds and by all three criteria of economic performance, Japan achieved an excellent economic performance throughout; Sweden, equally vulnerable, moved between above average and average.

Conversely we must take credit away from the United States for its above-average performance in 1980-84. Like Canada and Australia, it is among the least vulnerable to the oil shocks; it had to jump over only minor hurdles in 1975-84. Even so, during 1980-84 its annual real economic growth (0.9 percent) lagged behind that of both Japan (3.3 percent) and Sweden (1.4 percent). In this handicapping game, we can also suggest that the United Kingdom and the Netherlands, both with good energy positions, should have performed better than they did in the 1980-84 period.

In sum, among nineteen rich democracies and despite their handicaps, Japan and Austria rank excellent in general economic performance, 1980-84, and Sweden and West Germany rank good—consistent with our main theme regarding policy linkages, structures for bargaining, and their effects. The medium annual growth, low inflation, and medium unemployment of the United States in 1980-84 earns the same score (4 = above average) as Sweden, with its medium growth (1.4 percent vs. U.S. 0.9 percent), medium inflation (9.5 percent vs. U.S. 6.7 percent), and low unemployment (2.8 percent vs. U.S. 8.2 percent).

BIBLIOGRAPHY

Aaron, Henry J. 1978. *Politics and the Professors: The Great Society in Perspective.* Washington, D.C.: The Brookings Institution.

Adams, F. Gerald, and Klein, Lawrence R, eds. 1983. *Industrial Policies for Growth and Competitiveness*, vol. 1. Lexington, Mass.: Lexington Books, D. C. Heath and Co.

Addison, John T. 1981. "Incomes Policy: The Recent European Experience." In Fallick and Elliott, eds., pp. 156-86.

Aitken, Robert. 1986. "MSC, TVEI and Education in Perspective." *Political Quarterly* 57, 3: 231-35.

Balassa, Bela. 1985. "La politique industrielle socialiste." *Commentaire*, no. 30: 579-88.

Belfrage, Bengt, and Molleryd, Bengt. 1984. "Swedish Industrial Policy." In R. E. Driscoll and J. N. Behrman, eds., pp. 177-85.

Berger, Suzanne, ed. 1981. *Organizing Interests in Western Europe: Pluralism, Corporatism, and the Transformation of Politics.* Cambridge: Cambridge University Press. Cambridge Studies in Modern Political Economies.

Blank, Stephen. 1978. "Britain: The Politics of Foreign Economic Policy, the Domestic Economy, and the Problem of Pluralistic Stagnation." In *Between Power and Plenty: Foreign Economic Policies of Advanced Industrial States*, ed. Peter J. Katzenstein, pp. 89-137. Madison: University of Wisconsin Press.

Casey, Bernard, and Bruche, Geof. 1985. "Active Labor Market Policy: An International Overview." *Industrial Relations* 24 (Winter): 37-61.

Charnovitz, Steve. 1986. "Worker Adjustment: The Missing Ingredient in Trade Policy." *California Management Review* 28 (Winter): 156-73.

Cohen, Stephen S. 1977. *Modern Capitalist Planning: The French Model.* Berkeley: University of California Press. Enlarged paperback edition.

Cole, Robert E. 1971. *Japanese Blue Collar: The Changing Tradition.* Berkeley: University of California Press.

_____. 1979. *Work, Mobility and Participation: A Comparative Study of American and Japanese Industry.* Berkeley: University of California Press.

Curzon Price, Victoria. 1981. *Industrial Policies in the European Community.* London: Macmillan.

Daalder, Hans. 1974. "The Consociational Democracy Theme." *World Politics* 27: 604-21.

Driscoll, David D. 1982a. "Wage and Price Policy in Austria." In U.S. Congress, Joint Economic Committee, pp. 12-17.

_____. 1982b. "Wage and Price Policy in The Netherlands." In U.S. Congress, Joint Economic Committee, pp. 43-47.

Driscoll, Robert E., and Behrman, Jack N. eds. 1984. *National Industrial Policies.* Cambridge, Mass.: Oelgeschlager, Gunn and Hain.

Dunlop, John T. 1977. "Policy Decisions and Research in Economics and Industrial Relations." *Industrial and Labor Relations Review* 30: 275-82.

Enloe, Cynthia H. 1975. *The Politics of Pollution in a Comparative Perspective: Ecology and Power in Four Nations.* New York: David McKay.

Fallick, J. L., and Elliot, R. F., eds. 1981. *Incomes Policies, Inflation and Relative Pay.* London: George Allen and Unwin.

Flanagan, Robert J.; Soskice, David W.; and Ulman, Lloyd. 1983. *Unionism, Economic Stabilization, and Incomes Policies: European Experience.* Washington, D.C.: The Brookings Institution.

Flora, Peter, and Heidenheimer, Arnold J., eds. 1981. *The Development of Welfare States in Europe and America.* New Brunswick, N.J.: Transaction Books and the HIWED Project.

Fukushima, Kiyohiko. 1984. "Public Use of Private Interests: Japan's Industrial Policy." In R. E. Driscoll and J. N. Behrman, eds., pp. 73-84.

Gourevitch, Peter; Martin, Andrew; Ross, George; Allen, Christopher; Bornstein, Stephen; and Markovits, Andrei. 1984. *Unions and Economic Crisis: Britain, West Germany and Sweden.* London: George Allen and Unwin.

Haber, Wolfgang. 1982. "Industrial Policy, Trade Policy, and European Social Democracy." In Pinder, ed.

Hanley David L.; Kerr, A. P.; and Waites, N. H. 1979. *Contemporary France: Politics and Society Since 1975.* London: Routledge and Kegan Paul.

Haveman, Robert H. 1978. "The Dutch Social Employment Program." In *Creating Jobs: Public Employment Programs and Wage Subsidies*, ed. John L. Palmer, pp. 241-75. Washington, D.C.: The Brookings Institution.

_____. 1982. In *Technical Report Series*, T-82-1. U.S. National Commission for Employment Policy, January.

Haveman, Robert H., and Saks, Daniel H. 1985. "Transatlantic Lessons for Employment and Training Policy." *Industrial Relations* 24 (Winter): 20-36.

Haveman, Robert H., and Palmer, John L., eds. 1982. *Jobs for Disadvantaged Workers: The Economics of Employment Subsidies*. Washington, D.C.: The Brookings Institution.

Heidenheimer, Arnold J.; Heclo, Hugh; and Adams, Carolyn Teich. 1983. *Comparative Public Policy: The Politics of Social Choice in Europe and America*, 2d ed. New York: St. Martin's Press.

Henning, Roger. 1984. "Industrial Policy or Employment Policy? Sweden's Response to Unemployment." In Richardson and Henning, eds.

Hosomi, Takashi, and Okumura, Ariyoshi. 1982. "Japanese Industrial Policy." In Pinder, ed., pp. 123-57.

Houska, Joseph J. 1985. *Influencing Mass Political Behavior: Elites and Political Subcultures in the Netherlands and Austria*. Berkeley: Institute of International Studies. Research Series No. 60.

ILO (International Labor Organization). Various years. *Cost of Social Security*. Geneva.

Ingham, M. 1981. "Appendix—Incomes Policies: A Short History." In Fallick and Elliott, eds., pp. 264-80.

Janoski, Thomas. 1986. *The Political Economy of Unemployment: The Formation of Active Labor Market Policy in the United States and West Germany*. Unpublished Ph.D. dissertation, University of California, Berkeley.

Janowitz, Morris. 1976. *Social Control of the Welfare State*. New York: Elsevier Scientific Publishing.

Japan Institute of Labor. 1979a. *Employment and Employment Policy*. Tokyo. Japanese Industrial Relations Series, No. 1.

_____. 1979b. *Labor Unions and Labor-Management Relations*. Tokyo. Japanese Industrial Relations Series, No. 2.

Johanneson, Jan, and Schmid, Gunther. 1980. "The Development of Labour Market Policy in Sweden and in Germany: Competing or Convergent Models to Combat Unemployment?" *European Journal of Political Research* 8: 387-406.

Johnson, Chalmers. 1982. *MITI and the Japanese Miracle: The Growth of Industrial Policy 1925-1975*. Berkeley: University of California Press.

_____, ed. 1984. *The Industrial Policy Debate.* San Francisco: Institute for Contemporary Studies.

Juris, Hervey; Thompson, Mark; and Daniels, Wilbur, eds. 1985. *Industrial Relations in a Decade of Economic Change.* Madison, Wisc.: Industrial Relations Research Association.

Katzenstein, Peter J. 1984. *Corporatism and Change: Austria, Switzerland, and the Politics of Industry.* Ithaca: Cornell University Press.

_____. 1985. *Small States in World Markets: Industrial Policy in Europe.* Ithaca: Cornell University Press.

King, Anthony. 1975. "Overload: Problems of Governing in the 1970s." *Polititical Studies* 23: 284-96.

Kriesi, Hanspeter. 1982. "The Structure of the Swiss Political System." In Lehmbruch and Schmitter, eds., pp. 133-51.

Laroque, Pierre, ed. 1983. *The Social Institutions of France.* New York: Gordon and Breach Science Publishers.

Lawrence, Robert Z. 1984. *Can America Compete?* Washington, D.C.: The Brookings Institution.

Lehmbruch, Gerhard. 1979. "Liberal Corporatism and Party Government." In Schmitter and Lehmbruch, eds., pp. 147-84.

Lehmbruch, Gerhard, and Schmitter, Philippe C., eds. 1982. *Patterns of Corporatist Policy-Making.* Beverly Hills: Sage Publications.

Lester, Richard A. 1966. *Manpower Planning in a Free Society.* Princeton, N.J.: Princeton University Press.

Levine, Solomon B. 1983. "Japanese Industrial Relations: What Can We Import? Madison: University of Wisconsin, Industrial Relations Research Institute, reprint no. 250; from *Thirty-Sixth Annual National Conference on Labor*, ch. 2. New York: Matthew Bender and Co.

Lijphart, Arend. 1968. *The Politics of Accommodation: Pluralism and Democracy in the Netherlands.* Berkeley: University of California Press.

McArthur, Andrew A., and McGregor, Alan. 1986. "Training and Economic Development: National Versus Local Perspectives." *Political Quarterly* 57, 3: 246-55.

McKean, Margaret A. 1980. *Environmental Protest and Citizen Politics in Japan.* Berkeley: University of California Press.

Magaziner, Ira C., and Reich, Robert B. 1982. *Minding America's Business.* New York: Harcourt Brace Jovanovich.

Martin, Andrew. 1979. "The Dynamics of Change in a Keynesian Political Economy: The Swedish Case and Its Implications." In *State and Economy in Contemporary Capitalism,* ed. Colin Crouch. New York: St. Martin's Press.

_____. 1984. "Trade Unions in Sweden: Strategic Responses to Change and Crisis." In Gourevitch et al., pp. 190-359.

Moon, Jeremy. 1984. "The Responses of British Governments to Unemployment." In Richardson and Henning, eds., pp. 15-39.

Mouriaux, Marie-Françoise, and Mouriaux, René. 1984. "Unemployment Policy in France, 1976-82." In Richardson and Henning, eds., 148-66.

Nanto, Dick K. 1982. "Wage and Price Policy in Japan." In U.S. Congress, Joint Economic Committee, pp. 32-42.

OECD. 1963. *OECD Manpower Statistics 1950-62.* Paris.

_____. 1967a. *Manpower Policies and Problems in Austria.* Paris. OECD Reviews of Manpower and Social Policies, No. 5.

_____. 1967b. *Manpower and Social Policy in the Netherlands.* Paris. OECD Reviews of Manpower and Social Policies, No. 6.

_____. 1973a. *Manpower Policy in France.* Paris. OECD Reviews of Manpower and Social Policies, No. 12.

_____. 1973b. *Manpower Policy in Japan.* Paris. OECD Reviews of Manpower and Social Policies, No. 11.

_____. 1974. *Manpower Policy in Denmark.* Paris. OECD Reviews of Manpower and Social Policies, No. 14.

_____. 1975. *OECD Labor Force Statistics 1962-73.* Paris.

_____. 1979. *Policies for Apprenticeship.* Paris.

_____. 1985a. *OECD Labor Force Statistics 1960-83.* Paris.

_____. 1985b. *OECD Labor Force Statistics 1964-84.* Paris.

_____. 1986. *National Accounts 1960-1984.* Vol. 1: *Main Aggregates.* Paris.

Pempel, T. J., and Tsunekawa, K. 1979. "Corporatism Without Labor?" In Schmitter and Lehmbruch, eds., pp. 231-70.

Pencavel, John H. 1981. "The American Experience with Incomes Policies." In Fallick and Elliott, eds., pp. 155-86.

Pinder, John; Hosomi, Takashi; and Diebold, William. 1979. *Industrial Policy and the International Economy.* New York: The Trilateral Commission.

Pinder, John, ed. 1982. *National Industrial Strategies and the World Economy.* Totowa, N.J.: Allanheld, Osmun and Co.

Rees, Albert Jr. 1979. *The Economics of Work and Pay.* New York: Harper and Row.

Rehn, Gösta. 1985. "Swedish Active Labor Market Policy: Retrospect and Prospect." *Industrial Relations* 24 (Winter): 62-89.

Reubens, Beatrice. 1970. *The Hard to Employ: European Programs.* New York: Columbia University.

Richardson, Jeremy, and Henning, Roger, eds. 1984. *Unemployment: Policy Responses of Western Democracies.* London: Sage Publications.

Rohlen, Thomas P. 1979. "Permanent Employment Faces Recession, Slow Growth, Aging Labor Force." *Journal of Japanese Studies* 5, 2 (Summer): 235-72.

Rose, Richard, and Peters, Guy. 1978. *Can Governments Go Bankrupt?* New York: Basic Books.

Sabel, Charles F. 1984. "Industrial Reorganization and Social Democracy in Austria." *Industrial Relations* 23 (Fall): 334-61.

Scharpf, Fritz W. 1981. "The Political Economy of Inflation and Unemployment in Western Europe: An Outline." Wissenschaftszentrum Berlin: International Institute of Management. Discussion paper, IIM/LMP.

_____. 1983. "Economic and Institutional Constraints of Full-Employment Strategies: Sweden, Austria and West Germany (1973-1982)." Wissenschaftszentrum Berlin: International Institute of Management. Discussion paper, IIM/LMP 83-20.

Schmidt, Manfred G. 1982. "Does Corporatism Matter? Economic Crisis, Politics and Rates of Unemployment in Capitalist Democracies in the 1970's." In Lehmbruch and Schmitter, eds.

Schmitter, Philippe C. 1974. "Still the Century of Corporatism?" In *The New Corporatism: Social-Political Structures in the Iberian World*, ed. F. B. Pike and T. Stritch, pp. 85-131.

_____. 1981. "Interest Intermediation and Regime Governability in Contemporary Western Europe and North America." In Berger, ed.

Schmitter, Philippe C., and Lehmbruch, Gerhard, eds. 1979. *Trends Toward Corporatist Intermediation.* Beverly Hills: Sage Publications.

Sellier, François. 1985. "Economic Change and Industrial Relations in France." In Juris, Thompson, and Daniels, eds., pp. 177-209.

Sengenberger, Werner. 1984. "West German Employment Policy: Restoring Worker Competition." *Industrial Relations* 23 (Fall): 323-43.

Shimada, Haruo. 1977. "The Japanese Labor Market after the Oil Crisis: A Factual Report (II)." *Keio Economic Studies* 14, 2: 37-59.

_____. 1980. *Japanese Employment System.* Tokyo: Japan Institute of Labor. Japanese Industrial Relations Series, No. 6.

Soldwedel, Rüdiger. 1984. *Mehr Markt am Arbeitsmarkt.* Munich: Philosophia Verlag.

Streeck, Wolfgang. 1978. "Organizational Consequences of Corporatist Cooperation in West German Labor Unions: A Case Study." Berlin: International Institute of Management. Discussion paper.

_____. 1983. "Between Pluralism and Corporatism: German Business Associations and the State." *Journal of Public Policy* 3 (August): 265-83.

Taira, Koji, and Levine, Solomon B. 1985. "Japan's Industrial Relations: A Social Compact Emerges." In Juris, Thompson, and Daniels, eds., pp. 247-300.

United Nations, Department of Economic and Social Affairs. 1974. *World Energy Supplies: 1969-1972.* Statistical Papers. Series J, vol. 17. New York.

_____. 1979. *World Energy Supplies: 1973-1978.* Statistical Papers. Vol. 22. New York.

United Nations, Statistical Office. Various years. "International Tables." *Yearbook of National Accounts Statistics.* New York.

UN/ILO. Various years. *ILO Yearbook of Labor Force Statistics.* Geneva.

U.S. Congress, Joint Economic Committee. 1982. *Wage and Price Policies in Australia, Austria, Canada, the Netherlands, and West Germany.* Washington, D.C.: Government Printing Office.

Wagenhals, Gerhard. 1983. "Industrial Policy in the Federal Republic of Germany: A Survey." In Adams and Klein, eds., pp. 247-62.

Warnecke, Steven J., ed. 1978. *International Trade and Industrial Policies.* London: Macmillan.

Warnecke, Steven, and Suleiman, Ezra N., eds. 1975. *Industrial Policies in Western Europe.* New York: Praeger.

Wilensky, Harold L. 1965. "The Problems and Prospects of the Welfare State." In H. L. Wilensky and C. N. Lebeaux, *Industrial Society and Social Welfare,* pp. v-lii. Glencoe, Ill.: Free Press-Macmillan. Enlarged paperback edition.

_____. 1975. *The Welfare State and Equality: Structural and Ideological Roots of Public Expenditures.* Berkeley: University of California Press.

_____. 1976. *The "New Corporatism," Centralization, and the Welfare State.* London and Beverly Hills: Sage Publications. Contemporary Political Sociology Series, 06-020.

_____. 1981. "Leftism, Catholicism, and Democratic Corporatism: The Role of Political Parties in Recent Welfare State Development." In Flora and Heidenheimer, eds., pp. 345-82.

_____. 1983. "Political Legitimacy and Consensus: Missing Variables in the Assessment of Social Policy." In *Evaluating the Welfare State: Social and Political Perspectives,* ed. S. E. Spiro and E. Yuchtman-Yaar, pp. 51-74. New York: Academic Press.

_____ 1984. Preface to Japanese edition of *The Welfare State and Equality.* Tokyo: Bokutakusha Publishing.

_____. 1985. "Nothing Fails Like Success: The Evaluation Research Industry and Labor Market Policy." *Industrial Relations* 24 (Winter): 1-19.

_____. In preparation. *Tax and Spend: The Political Economy of Welfare in International Perspective.*

Wilensky, Harold L.; Luebbert, Gregory M.; Hahn, Susan Reed; and Jamieson, Adrienne M. 1985. *Comparative Social Policy: Theory, Methods, Findings.* Berkeley: Institute of International Studies. Research Series No. 62.

Wilson, Arlene. 1982. "Wage and Price Policy in West Germany." In U.S. Congress, Joint Economic Committee, pp. 48-56.

Wilson, Graham K. 1982. "Why Is There No Corporatism in the United States?" In Lehmbruch and Schmitter, eds., pp. 219-36.

Wolinetz, Steven B. 1983. "Neo-Corporatism and Industrial Policy in the Netherlands." Vancouver, B.C. Discussion paper for the Canadian Political Science Association, University of British Columbia, 6-8 June.

_____. 1985. "Wage Regulation in the Netherlands: The Rise and Fall of the Postwar Social Contract." Paper presented at the Council for European Studies Conference of Europeanists, Washington, D.C., 13-15 October.

Yamamura, Kozo. 1982. "Success that Soured: Administrative Guidance and Cartels in Japan." In *Policy and Trade Issues of the Japanese Economy*, ed. K. Yamamura. Seattle: University of Washington Press.

Zysman, John. 1983. *Governments, Markets, and Growth: Financial Systems and the Politics of Industrial Change*. Ithaca: Cornell University Press.

Zysman, John, and Tyson, Laura D'Andrea. 1984. "U.S. and Japanese Trade and Industrial Policies." Berkeley: Berkeley Roundtable on the International Economy, University of California. BRIE working paper.

INDEX

Active labor-market policy (ALMP), 3-5, 25-31, 55-63; apprenticeship as gray area, 28; country cases, 26-31, 55-63; definition, 3-5; ranking of countries, 26; sequence of policy initiation, 17, 20-1

Adjustment: for international competitiveness, 3; in relation to ALMP in various countries, 26-31; linked to economic and social policy, 20, 24-5

Austria, 1, 9; ALMP, 1, 19, 26, 28, 58-9; economic performance, 19; incomes policy, 1, 19, 41-3, 72-3; industrial policy, 19, 32, 35-6, 67-8; policy interdependence, 1, 18, 19, 48; social policy, 1, 19; type of political economy, 10, 15, 19

Bargaining structures, 1; corporatist without labor, 12-3, 48; democratic corporatist, 10-2, 48; least corporatist, 14-5

Business-government relations, 12-3, 48-9. See also Corporatist without labor; Democratic corporatist

Chronology of economic policies in eight countries, 55-79

Consensus, 10-1, 13, 15; requirements for, 10-1, 15. See also Social contract

Corporatism. See Corporatist without labor; Democratic corporatist

Corporatist without labor, 9, 12-4, 48-9; definition, 12-3; erosion of, 13; internal strains, 13-4; policy interdependence, 14, 17-8, 20, 21, 48-9. See also France; Japan

Democratic corporatist, 9, 10-2, 48, 50-1; definition, 10-1; internal strains, 15; policy implementation

advantages, 11-2, 15, 48, 50-1; policy interdependence, 17, 18, 48. See also Austria; Netherlands; Sweden; West Germany

Economic growth, 6; as measure of economic performance, 80; as measure of industrial policy success, 32; as component of industrial policy in various countries 32-40. See also Economic performance

Economic performance: and migrant workers, 81-3; and service jobs, 81-3; and women's work, 81-3; in corporatist without labor systems, 13, 19; increased employment as measure of, 81-3; in democratic corporatist systems, 11, 19; in least corporatist systems, 19; in relation to energy dependence, 83-4; in relation to policy success, 19; measures, 19, 80-1

Elites: awareness of policy interdependence, 1, 48; commitment to policy, 17

Employers, 11; associations, 10, 15, 48; centralization effects, 48

Energy dependence: as handicap, 33, 83-4; index of, 83-4; in relation to economic performance, 33, 83-4

Environmental pollution: Japanese response, 14; U.S. response, 14

France, 1, 11, 19; ALMP, 19, 21, 26, 29-30, 60-1; economic performance, 19; erosion of corporatism without labor, 13; incomes policy, 19, 42, 46; industrial policy 19, 20, 32, 33, 34, 48, 64-6; policy interdependence, 19, 20, 48, 50; social policy, 19, 20, 21; type of political economy, 12-3, 16, 19

HAROLD L. WILENSKY is Professor of Political Science in the Department of Political Science and Research Sociologist, Institute of Industrial Relations and Institute of International Studies, University of California, Berkeley.

LOWELL TURNER is a Social Science Research Council doctoral fellow, a research fellow at the Berkeley Roundtable on the International Economy, and a graduate student in political science at the University of California, Berkeley.

INTERNATIONAL AND AREA STUDIES
University of California at Berkeley

2223 Fulton Street, 3rd floor · · · · · · · · · · · · · · Berkeley, California 94720

Albert Fishlow, *Dean*

Recent books published by International and Area Studies include:

RESEARCH SERIES

71. *State & Welfare, USA/USSR: Contemporary Policy & Practice.*
Eds. Gail W. Lapidus & Guy E. Swanson. · · · · · · · · · · · · · · $22.50

72. *The Politics of Debt in Argentina, Brazil, & Mexico.*
Robert R. Kaufman. · · · · · · · · · · · · · · $9.50

73. *No Longer an American Lake? Alliance Problems in the South Pacific.*
Ed. John Ravenhill. · · · · · · · · · · · · · · $14.95

74. *Thinking New about Soviet "New Thinking."*
V. Kubálková & A. A. Cruickshank. · · · · · · · · · · · · · · $11.50

75. *Iberian Identity: Essays on the Nature of Identity in Portugal & Spain.*
Eds. Richard Herr & John H. R. Polt. · · · · · · · · · · · · · · $17.50

76. *Argentine Unions, the State & the Rise of Perón, 1930–1945.*
Joel Horowitz. · · · · · · · · · · · · · · $16.95

77. *The New Europe Asserts Itself: A Changing Role in International
Relations.* Eds. Beverly Crawford & Peter W. Schulze. · · · · · · · · · · · · · · $19.95

78. *The Soviet Sobranie of Laws: Problems of Codification and
Non-Publication.* Eds. Richard Buxbaum & Kathryn Hendley. · · · · · · · · · · · · · · $16.95

79. *Multilateralism in NATO: Shaping the Postwar Balance of Power,
1945–1961.* Steve Weber. · · · · · · · · · · · · · · $9.50

INSTITUTE OF INTERNATIONAL STUDIES:

POLICY PAPERS IN INTERNATIONAL AFFAIRS

35. *Large-Scale Foreign Policy Change: The Nixon Doctrine as History
& Portent.* Earl C. Ravenal. · · · · · · · · · · · · · · $8.50

36. *The Internationalization of Japan's Security Policy: Challenges &
Dilemmas for a Reluctant Power.* Michael G. L'Estrange. · · · · · · · · · · · · · · $5.95

37. *Why We Need Ideologies in U.S. Foreign Policy: Democratic Politics
& World Order.* Edward H. Alden & Franz Schurmann. · · · · · · · · · · · · · · $8.50

38. *Vanguard Parties & Revolutionary Change in the Third World: Soviet
Perspectives & Their Implications.* David E. Albright. · · · · · · · · · · · · · · $9.50

INSTITUTE OF EAST ASIAN STUDIES:

RESEARCH PAPERS AND POLICY STUDIES

33. *U.S.-Thailand Relations in a New International Era.*
Eds. Clark Neher and Wiwat Mungkandi. $20.00

34. *Korea-U.S. Relations in a Changing World.*
Eds. Robert Sutter and Han Sungjoo. $20.00

35. *Japan, ASEAN, and the United States.*
Eds. Harry H. Kendall and Clara Joewono. $20.00

36. *Asia in the 1990s: American and Soviet Perspectives.*
Eds. Robert A. Scalapino and Gennady I. Chufrin. $20.00

KOREA RESEARCH MONOGRAPHS

16. *North Korea in Transition.*
Eds. Chong-Sik Lee and Yoo Se-Hee. $12.00

CHINA RESEARCH MONOGRAPHS

36. *China's Education Reform in the 1980s: Policies, Issues, and Historical Perspectives.* Suzanne Pepper. $12.00

37. *Building a Nation-State: China after Forty Years.*
Ed. Joyce K. Kallgren. $12.00

INDOCHINA RESEARCH MONOGRAPHS

5. *The Bunker Papers: Reports to the President from Vietnam, 1967–1973.*
Ed. Douglas Pike.   (3 vols.) $35.00

**CENTER FOR SLAVIC AND EAST EUROPEAN STUDIES/
BERKELEY-STANFORD PROGRAM IN SOVIET STUDIES**

Analyzing the Gorbachev Era: Working Papers of the Students of the Berkeley-Stanford Program. $8.00

Can Gorbachev's Reforms Succeed?
Ed. George W. Breslauer. $12.95

Steeltown, USSR: Glasnost, Destalinization & Perestroika in the Provinces.
Stephen Kotkin. $6.00